Selections From
FRENCH POETRY

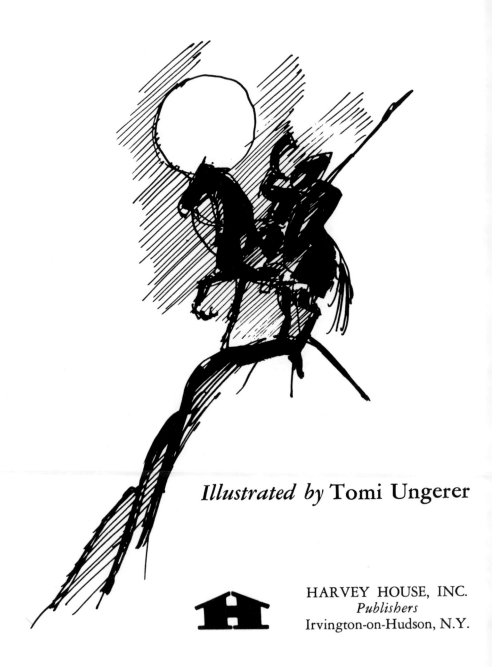

Illustrated by Tomi Ungerer

HARVEY HOUSE, INC.
Publishers
Irvington-on-Hudson, N.Y.

Selections
From
FRENCH
POETRY

by Kenneth F. Canfield

HARVEY HOUSE, INC., *Publishers*
Irvington-on-Hudson, New York

Library of Congress Catalog Card Number: 65-14631

Manufactured in the United States of America

Foreword

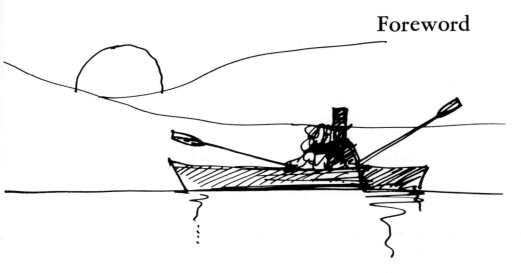

Recently I attended a symposium on "Dante and His Translators" in which a group of Dante scholars proceeded, as I expected, to pick out some of the most famous lines in the *Divine Comedy* in order to show how inadequate was their English translation. *Traduttore, traditore!* It is axiomatic, I believe, that poetry, especially great poetry, is untranslatable. It is at best "prose run mad," wrote Alexander Pope, and it has been said with a great deal of truth that, in a poem, pure poetry is that part which escapes translation.

A native Frenchman is poorly qualified to pass judgment on an English translation of French poetry. An anthology such as the present one includes, by definition, the most famous poems of his own literature, a good many of which he has known by heart since his childhood. As a result, when he listens to the foreign version of a piece so familiar to him, he cannot help being aware of the "sad incompetence"—to borrow Wordsworth's phrase—of the English idiom faithfully to render his own. He is likely, therefore, to conclude that the translator has turned a good poem into a bad one. His experience—*mutatis mutandis*—is akin to that of the music lover exposed to a jazzed-up rendering of a favorite adagio. He forgets, of course, that the translator is not addressing himself to a Frenchman, but to those readers who do not understand the original.

It should be said, however, that the translator—I mean the translator worth his salt—who chooses to translate great poetry rather than "celle qui n'est que de la prose où les vers se sont mis," must realize that the quality of his work will, in the final analysis, be judged by his peers, I mean by truly bilingual critics who will scrutinize it with the severity of a teacher of Classics grading an undergraduate's Latin composition. An anthology like this one is a courageous undertaking. Its author is a teacher of French of long standing and he knows better than anyone that there will be carping critics who will pounce with delight on this or that poem and point out how inferior it is to the original. Their task will be all the easier since both texts are printed side by side by Mr. Canfield, who has not feared to offer to their barbs a few translations of his own.

Needless to say, with such a wealth of poetry, covering six centuries, there are bound to be differences in the quality of the various translations. Some are quite felicitous, others less so. As was to be expected, it is the best of the originals which have most successfully defied the translators, but all of them deserve their share of applause. All would be justified in saying to their French model in the words of the lover of Cynara:

"I have been faithful to thee . . . in my fashion!"

VINCENT GUILLOTON

Lawrenceville, New Jersey
June, 1965

Preface

Selections from French Poetry was compiled to interest many people, from high school student to college graduate. The book's bilingual format serves several purposes: For people whose French has become vague from long disuse, a reading of the English version on the facing page will be an agreeable reminder and may save much searching for individual words in a dictionary. Or a diligent scholar whose French is rather good may want to take a quick glance to find an occasional phrase or interpretation. The college student interested in stylistics should have a field day analyzing the problems involved in the translation of poetry. Students of world literature in English translation by using this bilingual edition can, if they have an elementary knowledge of French pronunciation, enjoy the rhythm and music of the original French while depending on the English version for a professional approximation of a poem's meaning and style.

In the sixty-three poems one finds the greatest variety—from the fifteenth century almost to the present moment. Naturally, in a literature as rich and as vast as that of France, some authors and some favorite selections have had to be omitted from a book of this convenient size. No meaning should be read into these omissions other than the restrictions of space. The poems are, in general, of medium difficulty. Many are rather simple, in both form and content, for English-speaking students of French. Some are old favorites taught in second and third semester college courses and in second and third year high school classes. The most difficult poems of the Symbolist and Surrealist movements have been omitted. Apollinaire, Éluard, and Prévert are included with the hope that these few examples of fairly recent poetry may encourage readers to explore further the French poetry written between the two World Wars and since the second.

As for the English translations, the editor readily admits that no translation of French poetry into English does justice to the original. The basic differences between a Romance language and a Germanic one make this doubly so. But it is a fascinating game to try one's hand at, and it is exciting to see how ingenious some translators have been. Many a poet has been tempted by the process. The translations used in this edition have been carefully sought out and are, generally speaking, excellent. Where no professional translation appeared available, the editor has attempted an unrhymed English version in which he has tried to remain reasonably close to the spirit of the original.

Of necessity the biographical notes are brief and incomplete. They are not written for the specialist. Just as the poems are presented to kindle or rekindle an interest in French poetry, in the same way the little sketches have been included to make readers want to find out more about the authors, their lives, and their work.

K.F.C.

Acknowledgments

The editor and the publishers are grateful for the cooperation of those individuals and publishers who granted permission to use their copyrighted material. Every effort has been made to trace and to acknowledge properly all copyright owners. If any acknowledgment has been inadvertently omitted, the publishers will be pleased to make the necessary correction in the next printing.

"Rondeau," "The Flute," "The Lake," "The Sower," "Sensations," and "Wind From the Sea," translated from the French by Wilfrid Thorley, in *Fleurs-de-Lys.* William Heinemann, Publisher, London, England.

"Ballade of Small Talk," from *The Complete Works of François Villon,* translated by Anthony Bonner. © Copyright 1960 by Bantam Books, Inc. and reprinted by permission of the Publisher. All Rights Reserved.

"Life's Roses," translated by Curtis Hidden Page, in *Songs and Sonnets of Pierre de Ronsard.* Reprinted by permission of Houghton Mifflin Company, Boston.

"To Cassandra" and "As on the Branch," translated from the French by E. J. Dennis, in *Salute to Ronsard.* Reprinted by permission of The Robin Press, Bell Garth, Lund, Driffield, Yorkshire, England.

"Nostalgia," reprinted by permission of the translator, Rudolf Gottfried, from *Six Sonnets from Les Regrets* by Joachim du Bellay.

"To Madame du Châtelet," "Tristesse," and "Stained Glass," reprinted with permission of the copyright owners, the Regents of the University of Wisconsin, from W. F. Giese, *French Lyrics in English Verse,* 1946, the University of Wisconsin Press.

"The Roses of Sa'adi," copyright © 1954 by Barbara Howes. Reprinted from *Light and Dark* by Barbara Howes by permission of Wesleyan University Press.

"The Horn," "The Elephants," "Head of a Faun," and "Vowels," translated from the French by Alan Conder, in *A Treasury of French Poetry.* Cassell and Company Ltd., London.

"Mimi Pinson," translated from the French by Jessie Hendry McEwan, in *Short Anthology of Translations.* William MacLellan, Publisher, Glasgow.

"Epitaph," translated from the French by Brian Hill, in *Fortune's Fool.* Reprinted by permission of the translator.

Contents

* TRANSLATION BY THE EDITOR

* TRANSLATION BY THE EDITOR

Rondeau

Tyme hath throwne downe the robe he bare
Of winde and cold and chillye rayne,
And nowe with sunbeams cleare agayne
In lordlye raiment doth he fare.

Each beast and birde doth nowe declare
Harsh-voiced or smoothe the tidynges playne:
Tyme hath throwne downe the robe he bare
Of winde and cold and chillye rayne.

Nowe fountaynes, streams and brookes repair
Their sheeny floods that downward drayne
With gold and silver in their trayne;
All thynges new vesture nowe doe weare:
Tyme hath throwne downe the robe he bare.

Translated by WILFRID THORLEY

Nephew of Charles VI and father of Louis XII, Charles d'Orléans (1391-1465) spent twenty-five years in England after being taken prisoner at Agincourt. Returning to France in 1440, he lived luxuriously in his château at Blois. His poetry, while facile and traditional, has a certain elegance and grace which have made it live.

Rondeau

Le temps a laissé son manteau
De vent, de froidure et de pluie,
Et s'est vêtu de broderie,
De soleil luisant, clair et beau.

Il n'y a bête ni oiseau,
Qu'en son jargon ne chante ou crie :
« Le temps a laissé son manteau
De vent, de froidure et de pluie.»

Rivière, fontaine et ruisseau
Portent en livrée jolie
Gouttes d'argent, d'orfèvrerie ;
Chacun s'habille de nouveau.
Le temps a laissé son manteau.

Ballad of Old-Time Ladies

Tell me where, in what land of shade,
Bides fair Flora of Rome, and where
Are Thaïs and Archipiade,
Cousins-german of beauty rare,
And Echo, more than mortal fair,
That, when one calls by river-flow,
Or marish, answers out of the air?
But what is become of last year's snow?

Where did the learn'd Heloïsa vade,
For whose sake Abelard might not spare
(Such dole for love on him was laid)
Manhood to lose and a cowl to wear?
And where is the queen who willed whilere
That Buridan, tied in a sack, should go
Floating down Seine from the turret-stair?
But what is become of last year's snow?

Blanche, too, the lily-white queen, that made
Sweet music as if she a siren were;
Broad-foot Bertha; and Joan the maid,
The good Lorrainer, the English bare
Captive to Rouen and burned her there;
Beatrix, Eremburge, Alys,—lo!
Where are they, Virgin debonair?
But what is become of last year's snow?

Ballade des Dames du Temps Jadis

Dites-moi où, n'en quel pays,
Est Flora, la belle Romaine,
Archipiada, ni Thaïs
Qui fut sa cousine germaine,
Écho parlant quand bruit on mène
Dessus rivière ou sus étang,
Qui beauté eut trop plus qu'humaine.
Mais où sont les neiges d'antan?

Où est la très sage Héloïs,
Pour qui fut châtré, puis moine,
Pierre Abélard à Saint-Denis?
Pour son amour eut cet essoyne.
Semblablement où est la reine
Qui commanda que Buridan
Fût jeté en un sac en Seine?
Mais où sont les neiges d'antan?

La reine Blanche comme lis,
Qui chantait à voix de sirène;
Berte au grand pied, Béatrix, Alix;
Haremburgis qui tint le Maine,
Et Jehanne, la bonne Lorraine,
Qu'Anglais brûlèrent à Rouen,
Où sont-elz, où, Vierge souveraine?
Mais où sont les neiges d'antan?

ENVOI

Prince, you may question how they fare
This week, or liefer this year, I trow:
Still shall the answer this burden bear,
But what is become of last year's snow?

Translated by JOHN PAYNE

François Villon (1431-1462?): One of the most colorful personalities in French literature. Orphaned early and poor, helped by a priest whose name he adopted, Villon took the university degree of maître-ès-arts *and was made* licencié, *but the wildly bohemian life of Paris fascinated him and Villon spent much time evading prosecution for murder and theft. Consumed by the thought of death, Villon is a modern writer, himself the subject of his poetry, and his own emotions—from sadness to raillery—are those of his writings.*

ENVOI

Prince, n'enquérez de semaine
Où elles sont, ni de cet an,
Que ce refrain ne vous remaine:
Mais où sont les neiges d'antan?

Ballade of Small Talk

I know flies in the milk,
I know men by their clothes,
I know good from bad weather,
I know fruit by its color,
I know trees by their sap,
I know when all is the same,
I know who's busy or idle,
I know all, save myself.

I know doublets by their collars,
I know monks by their robes,
I know masters by their servants,
I know nuns by their veils,
I know con-men by their slang,
I know fools fed on cheese,
I know wine by its cask,
I know all, save myself.

I know horses and mules,
I know the load they can carry,
I know Marys and Janes,
I know counting and adding,
I know visions and sleep,
I know heresies of Hussites,
I know the power of Rome,
I know all, save myself.

Prince, I know all, in short,
I know pink cheeks from wan,
I know Death all-devouring,
I know all, save myself.

Translated by ANTHONY BONNER

Des Menus Propos

Je connais bien mouches en lait,
Je connais à la robe l'homme,
Je connais le beau temps du laid,
Je connais au pommier la pomme,
Je connais l'arbre à voir la gomme,
Je connais quand tout est de même,
Je connais qui besogne ou chôme,
Je connais tout fors que moi-même.

Je connais pourpoint au collet,
Je connais le moine à la gonne,
Je connais le maître au varlet,
Je connais au voile la nonne,
Je connais quand pipeur jargonne,
Je connais fous nourris de crème,
Je connais le vin à la tonne,
Je connais tout fors que moi-même.

Je connais cheval et mulet,
Je connais leur charge et leur somme,
Je connais Biétrix et Belet,
Je connais jet qui nombre et somme,
Je connais vision et somme,
Je connais la faute des Bohèmes,
Je connais le pouvoir de Rome,
Je connais tout fors que moi-même.

Prince, je connais tout en somme.
Je connais coulourés et blèmes,
Je connais mort qui tout consomme,
Je connais tout fors que moi-même.

Life's Roses

When you are very old, by the hearth's glare,
At candle-time, spinning and winding thread,
You'll sing my lines, and say, astonishèd:
Ronsard made these for me, when I was fair.

Then not a servant even, with toil and care
Almost out-worn, hearing what you have said,
Shall fail to start awake and lift her head
And bless your name with deathless praise fore'er.

My bones shall lie in earth, and my poor ghost
Take its long rest where Love's dark myrtles thrive.
You, crouching by the fire, old, shrunken, grey,

Shall rue your proud disdain and my love lost. . . .
Nay, hear me, love! Wait not to-morrow! Live,
And pluck life's roses, oh! today, to-day.

Translated by CURTIS HIDDEN PAGE

Pierre de Ronsard (1524-1585) is the chief poet of the Pléiade, the sixteenth-century group in France that wanted to draw from Greek, Latin, and Italian poets the inspiration for truly great French writing. Ronsard loved life and the beauty of things with a pagan and sensual voluptuousness, never forgetting, however, the all too certain approach of death. His finest lyric works are the simple odes and sonnets in which his own loves and reveries are mirrored.

Sonnet pour Hélène

Quand vous serez bien vieille, au soir à la chandelle,
Assise auprès du feu, dévidant et filant,
Direz chantant mes vers, en vous émerveillant:
Ronsard me célébrait du temps que j'étais belle.

Lors vous n'aurez servante oyant telle nouvelle,
Déjà sous le labeur à demi sommeillant,
Qui au bruit de mon nom ne s'aille réveillant,
Bénissant votre nom de louange immortelle.

Je serai sous la terre, et fantôme sans os,
Par les ombres myrteux je prendrai mon repos;
Vous serez au foyer une vieille accroupie,

Regrettant mon amour et votre fier dédain.
Vivez, si m'en croyez, n'attendez à demain;
Cueillez dès aujourd'hui les roses de la vie.

As on the Branch

As on the branch in May one sees the rose
In her fresh beauty, touched at the dawn with dew,
Make heaven jealous of her eager hue,
Stir in the sky the envy of her foes:

In tear-dropped petals, grace and love repose,
Her fragrance wafts the copse and garden through:
Yet rain and sun assail her to ensue
Her death in languor, as her leaves unclose.

So, in your first and youthful loveliness,
When earth and heaven alike your name did bless,
Fate struck you down, and here your dust reposes.

For obsequies receive my tears and weeping,
This vase of milk, this basket of flowers, that sleeping
In death, as e'er in life, you be of roses.

Translated by E. J. DENNIS

Sonnet pour Marie

Comme on voit sur la branche au mois de mai la rose
En sa belle jeunesse, en sa première fleur,
Rendre le ciel jaloux de sa vive couleur,
Quand l'aube de ses pleurs au point du jour l'arrose,

La grâce dans sa feuille, et l'amour se repose,
Embaumant les jardins et les arbres d'odeur;
Mais battue ou de pluie, ou d'excessive ardeur
Languissante, elle meurt, feuille à feuille déclose.

Ainsi en ta première et jeune nouveauté,
Quand le ciel et la terre honoraient ta beauté,
La Parque t'a tuée, et cendre tu reposes.

Pour obsèques reçois mes larmes et mes pleurs,
Ce vase plein de lait, ce panier plein de fleurs,
Afin que vif et mort ton corps ne soit que roses.

To Cassandra

Come see, my darling, if the Rose,
Whose robe of purple did unclose
When Sun at dawn began to shine,
Has lost, of her empurpled dress,
Aught of her form of loveliness,
Or of her colour fair as thine.

Alas! my darling, see how soon,
In one short morn and afternoon,
Her beauties dropped and scattered wide!
O cruel Nature, harsh of power,
Who dost not suffer such a flower
To live from dawn till eventide!

Heed me, my darling, while 'tis spring,
And while thy life is blossoming
In all its greenness fresh arrayed;
Use, use thy youth while yet it blows:
Old age to thee, as to the Rose,
Will make thy beauty shrink and fade.

Translated by E. J. DENNIS

À Cassandre

Mignonne, allons voir si la rose
Qui ce matin avait déclose
Sa robe de pourpre au soleil
A point perdu cette vesprée
Les plis de sa robe pourprée,
Et son teint au vôtre pareil.

Las! voyez comme en peu d'espace,
Mignonne, elle a dessus la place,
Las! las! ses beautés laissé choir!
O vraiment marâtre Nature,
Puisqu'une telle fleur ne dure
Que du matin jusques au soir!

Donc, si vous me croyez, mignonne,
Tandis que votre âge fleuronne
En sa plus verte nouveauté,
Cueillez, cueillez votre jeunesse:
Comme à cette fleur, la vieillesse
Fera ternir votre beauté.

Epitaph to His Soul

Dear, sweet little soul of Ronsard,
Delicate, gentle that you are,
Honored tenant of my person,
You go downward, o so feeble,
Pale, so thin, and so all alone
Into the cold realm of the dead.
Yet artless, plain, without remorse,
For murder, poison or malice,
Disdaining favors and treasures
So held in awe by the masses.
Trav'ler, I said, be on your way,
Trouble not my repose; I sleep.

Translated by K. F. C.

Épitaphe à son Âme

Âmelette Ronsardelette,
Mignonnelette, doucelette,
Très chère hôtesse de mon corps,
Tu descends là-bas faiblelette,
Pâle, maigrelette, seulette,
Dans le froid royaume des morts;
Toutefois simple, sans remords,
De meurtre, poison, ou rancune,
Méprisant faveurs et trésors
Tant enviés par la commune.
Passant, j'ai dit: suis ta fortune,
Ne trouble mon repos: je dors.

Perfection

If here our life be briefer than a day
In Time Eternal, if the circling year
Drive on our days never to reappear,
If birth be but the prelude to decay,

What think you, soul, incarcerate in clay?
Why are you glad, at our dark daylight here,
If for the flight to an abode more clear
Your strong wings are well feathered to upstay?

There, is the good that every mind desires,
There, rest whereunto all the world aspires,
There love is, there of pleasure too full worth:

There, O my soul, led on to Heaven's last height,
The very self of Beauty in thy sight
Shall seem the image worshipped upon earth.

Translated by GEORGE WYNDHAM

Next to Ronsard, Joachim du Bellay (1522-1560) is the most important poet of the Pléiade. Both men studied at the Collège de Coqueret in Paris under Dorat. Later, in 1549, Du Bellay wrote the manifesto of the Pléiade, the famous Défense et Illustration de la Langue Française. *Always in delicate health, the poet nevertheless longed to make his mark in the world and believed himself launched in the field of diplomacy when he accompanied his cousin, Cardinal Jean du Bellay, on a mission to Rome in 1553. But his diplomatic life in the Eternal City was not what he had dreamed, and he soon yearned to be back in Anjou. The sonnet,* L'Amour du Clocher (Nostalgia), *tells of his homesickness. Lyré (Liré) is the village near the author's family home.*

L'Idéal

Si notre vie est moins qu'une journée
En l'éternel, si l'an qui fait le tour
Chasse nos jours sans espoir de retour,
Si périssable est toute chose née,

Que songes-tu, mon âme emprisonée?
Pourquoi te plaît l'obscur de notre jour,
Si, pour voler en un plus clair séjour,
Tu as au dos l'aile bien empennée?

Là, est le bien que tout esprit désire,
Là, le repos où tout le monde aspire,
Là, est l'amour, là, le plaisir encore.

Là, ô mon âme, au plus haut ciel guidée,
Tu y pourras reconnaître l'Idée
De la beauté, qu'en ce monde j'adore.

Nostalgia

Happy who like Ulysses homeward rides,
Or goes like Jason from the dragon's den,
And once arrived among his countrymen,
With them in deep sobriety abides.

Alas, when shall I see the smoke that glides
So quietly from village hearths? and when
Shall I the little courtyard see again
Which is my kingdom and so much besides?

I love my fathers' home and household gods
Far more than Rome's great arrogant façades;
Love the fine slate far more than marble's hue;

More than the Tiber love my Loire of Gaul,
More than the Palatine my Lyré small,
More than salt air the sweetness of Anjou.

Translated by RUDOLF GOTTFRIED

L'Amour du Clocher

Heureux qui, comme Ulysse, a fait un beau voyage,
Ou comme celui-là qui conquit la toison,
Et puis est retourné, plein d'usage et raison,
Vivre entre ses parents le reste de son âge!

Quand reverrai-je hélas, de mon petit village
Fumer la cheminée, et en quelle saison
Reverrai-je le clos de ma pauvre maison,
Qui m'est une province, et beaucoup davantage?

Plus me plaît le séjour qu'ont bâti mes aïeux
Que des palais romains le front audacieux,
Plus que le marbre dur me plaît l'ardoise fine,

Plus mon Loire gaulois que le Tibre latin,
Plus mon petit Lyré que le mont Palatin,
Et plus que l'air marin la douceur angevine.

The Raven and the Fox

Perched on a lofty oak,
  Sir Raven held a lunch of cheese;
Sir Fox, who smelt it in the breeze
  Thus to the holder spoke:—
  "Ha! how do you do, Sir Raven?
Well, your coat, sir, is a brave one!
  So black and glossy, on my word, sir,
  With voice to match, you were a bird, sir,
Well fit to be the Phoenix of these days."
Sir Raven, overset with praise,
  Must show how musical his croak.
Down fell the luncheon from the oak;
Which snatching up, Sir Fox thus spoke:—
  "The flatterer, my good sir,
  Aye liveth on his listener;
Which lesson, if you please,
  Is doubtless worth the cheese."
Somewhat too late, Sir Raven thought
Himself a fool to be so caught.

Translated by ELIZUR WRIGHT, JR.

Jean de La Fontaine (1621-1695) is often considered the greatest fabulist of all time. His superiority over his predecessors lies largely in his dramatic sense and in the care with which he develops every element of the drama in his fables. A classicist by instinct, La Fontaine is nevertheless independent in versification and vocabulary, and, by bringing his own experiences and feelings into his writings, he makes himself a lyric poet of the classical period.

Le Corbeau et le Renard

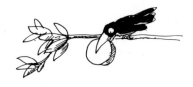

Maître Corbeau, sur un arbre perché,
　　Tenait en son bec un fromage.
Maître Renard, par l'odeur alléché,
　　Lui tint à peu près ce langage:
　　« Hé bonjour, Monsieur du Corbeau,
Que vous êtes joli! que vous me semblez beau!
　　Sans mentir, si votre ramage
　　Se rapporte à votre plumage,
Vous êtes le phénix des hôtes de ces bois.»
À ces mots le Corbeau ne se sent pas de joie;
　　Et, pour montrer sa belle voix,
Il ouvre un large bec, laisse tomber sa proie.
Le Renard s'en saisit, et dit: « Mon bon Monsieur,
　　Apprenez que tout flatteur
　　Vit au dépens de celui qui l'écoute.
Cette leçon vaut bien un fromage, sans doute.»
　　Le Corbeau, honteux et confus,
Jura, mais un peu tard, qu'on ne l'y prendrait plus.

The Oak and the Reed

The oak, one day, addressed the reed:—
"To you ungenerous indeed
Has nature been, my humble friend,
With weakness aye obliged to bend.
The smallest bird that flits in air
Is quite too much for you to bear;
     The slightest wind that wreaths the lake
     Your ever-trembling head doth shake.
The while, my towering form
Dares with the mountain top
The solar blaze to stop,
     And wrestle with the storm.
What seems to you the blast of death,
To me is but a zephyr's breath.
Beneath my branches had you grown,
     That spread far round their friendly bower,
     Less suffering would your life have known,
     Defended from the tempest's power.
     Unhappily, you oftenest show
     In open air your slender form.
Along the marshes, wet and low,
That fringe the kingdom of the storm.
To you, declare I must,
Dame Nature seems unjust."
Then modestly replied the reed,
"Your pity, sir, is kind indeed,
But wholly needless for my sake.
     The wildest wind that ever blew
     Is safe to me, compared with you.
I bend, indeed, but never break.

Le Chêne et le Roseau

Le chêne, un jour, dit au Roseau:
« Vous avez bien sujet d'accuser la nature;
Un roitelet pour vous est un pesant fardeau;
Le moindre vent qui d'aventure
Fait rider la face de l'eau,
Vous oblige à baisser la tête;
Cependant que mon front, au Caucase pareil,
Non content d'arrêter les rayons du soleil,
Brave l'effort de la tempête.
Tout vous est aquilon, tout me semble zéphyr.
Encor si vous naissiez à l'abri du feuillage
Dont je couvre le voisinage,
Vous n'auriez pas tant à souffrir,
Je vous défendrais de l'orage;
Mais vous naissez le plus souvent
Sur les humides bords des royaumes du vent.
La nature envers vous me semble bien injuste.
— Votre compassion, lui répondit l'arbuste,
Part d'un bon naturel; mais quittez ce souci:
Les vents me sont moins qu'à vous redoutables;
Je plie, et ne romps pas. Vous avez jusqu'ici
Contre leurs coups épouvantables
Résisté sans courber le dos;
Mais attendons la fin.» Comme il disait ces mots,
Du bout de l'horizon accourt avec furie
Le plus terrible des enfants
Que le Nord eût portés jusque-là dans ses flancs.

Thus far, I own, the hurricane
Has beat your sturdy back in vain;
But wait the end." Just at the word,
The tempest's hollow voice was heard.
The North sent forth her fiercest child,
Dark, jagged, pitiless, and wild.
The oak, erect, endured the blow;
The reed bowed gracefully and low.
But, gathering up its strength once more,
In greater fury than before,
The savage blast
O'erthrew, at last,
That proud, old, sky-encircled head,
Whose feet entwined the empire of the dead!

Translated by ELIZUR WRIGHT, JR.

L'arbre tient bon; le Roseau plie.
Le vent redouble ses efforts
Et fait si bien qu'il déracine
Celui de qui la tête au ciel était voisine
Et dont les pieds touchaient à l'empire des morts.

The Cobbler and the Financier

A cobbler sang from morn till night;
      'Twas sweet and marvelous to hear.
His trills and quavers told the ear
      Of more contentment and delight,
Enjoyed by that laborious wight,
      Than e'er enjoyed the sages seven,
      Or any mortals short of heaven.
His neighbor, on the other hand,
With gold in plenty at command,
      But little sang, and slumbered less—
      A financier of great success.
If e'er he dozed at break of day,
      The cobbler's song drove sleep away;
      And much he wished that Heaven had made
Sleep a commodity of trade,
In market sold, like food and drink,
      So much an hour, so much a wink.
At last, our songster did he call
To meet him in his princely hall.
      Said he, "Now, honest Gregory,
      What may your yearly earnings be?"
      "My yearly earnings! faith, good sir,
I never go, at once, so far,"
The cheerful cobbler said,
And queerly scratched his head,—
      "I never reckon in that way,
But cobble on from day to day,
Content with daily bread."
"Indeed! Well, Gregory, pray
What may your earnings be per day?"
"Why, sometimes more and sometimes less.

Le Savetier et le Financier

Un Savetier chantait du matin jusqu'au soir;
      C'était merveilles de le voir,
Merveilles de l'ouïr; il faisait des passages,
        Plus content qu'aucun des sept sages.
Son voisin, au contraire, étant tout cousu d'or,
      Chantait peu, dormait moins encor;
      C'était un homme de finance.
Si, sur le point du jour, parfois il sommeillait,
Le Savetier alors en chantant l'éveillait;
      Et le Financier se plaignait
      Que les soins de la Providence
N'eussent pas au marché fait vendre le dormir,
      Comme le manger et le boire.
      En son hôtel il fait venir
Le chanteur, et lui dit: « Or ça, sire Grégoire,
Que gagnez-vous par an? — Par an? Ma foi, Monsieur,
      Dit, avec un ton de rieur,
Le gaillard Savetier, ce n'est point ma manière
De compter de la sorte; et je n'entasse guère
      Un jour sur l'autre; il suffit qu'à la fin
      J'attrape le bout de l'année;
      Chaque jour amène son pain.
— Eh bien, que gagnez-vous, dites-moi, par journée?
— Tantôt plus, tantôt moins: le mal est que toujours
(Et sans cela nos gains seraient assez honnêtes),
Le mal est que dans l'an s'entremêlent des jours
      Qu'il faut chômer; on nous ruine en fêtes;
L'une fait tort à l'autre; et Monsieur le curé
De quelque nouveau saint charge toujours son prône.»
Le Financier, riant de sa naïveté,
Lui dit: « Je vous veux mettre aujourd'hui sur le trône.

The worst of all, I must confess,
(And but for which our gains would be
A pretty sight, indeed, to see,)
Is that the days are made so many
In which we cannot earn a penny—
The sorest ill the poor man feels:
They tread upon each other's heels,
Those idle days of holy saints!
And though the year is shingled o'er,
The parson keeps a-finding more!"
With smiles provoked by these complaints
Replied the lordly financier,
"I'll give you better cause to sing.
These hundred pounds I hand you here
Will make you happy as a king.
Go, spend them with a frugal heed;
They'll long supply your every need."
The cobbler thought the silver more
Than he had ever dreamed before,
The mines for ages could produce,
Or world, with all its people, use.
He took it home and there did hide,
And with it laid his joy aside.
No more of song, no more of sleep,
But cares, suspicions in their stead,
And false alarms, by fancy fed.
His eyes and ears their vigil keep,
And not a cat can tread the floor
But seems a thief slipped through the door.
At last, poor man!
Up to the financier he ran,—
Then in his morning nap profound:
"O, give me back my songs," cried he,
"And sleep, that used so sweet to be,
And take the money, every pound!"

Translated by ELIZUR WRIGHT, JR.

Prenez ces cent écus; gardez-les avec soin,
Pour vous en servir au besoin.»
Le Savetier crut voir tout l'argent que la terre
Avait, depuis plus de cent ans,
Produit pour l'usage des gens.
Il retourne chez lui; dans sa cave il enserre
L'argent, et sa joie à la fois.
Plus de chant: il perdit la voix,
Du moment qu'il gagna ce qui cause nos peines.
Le sommeil quitta son logis;
Il eut pour hôte les soucis,
Les soupçons, les alarmes vaines;
Tout le jour, il avait l'oeil au guet; et la nuit,
Si quelque chat faisait du bruit,
Le chat prenait l'argent. A la fin le pauvre homme
S'en courut chez celui qu'il ne réveillait plus:
« Rendez-moi, lui dit-il, mes chansons et mon somme,
Et reprenez vos cent écus.»

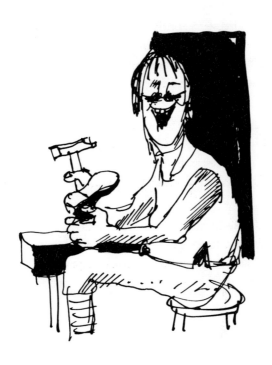

To Madame du Châtelet

If you would have me love you still,
Bring back to me the age of love,
And while I totter down the hill
Let evening a new daybreak prove.

From bowers where Bacchus plucks the grape
And Cupid bends his twanging bow,
Old Father Time, that grisly shape,
With threatening gesture bids me go.

Then let me bow to Time's fell rage
And from his spite some profit wring:
Who spurns the wisdom of old age
Bears all the burdens age doth bring.

Let's leave to youth love's sprightly charms,
Love's bliss, love's dainty melancholy,
Let our first years know love's alarms,
But let our last be free from folly!

Alas! must you forever flee,
Illusions sweet and dear delights,
That once made life so fair to me,
That charmed my days and thrilled my nights?

We die not once, but twice, alas!
Ceasing to love and to be loved—
What pang can such a grief surpass,
And when has death so painful proved?

Stances à Madame du Châtelet

Si vous voulez que j'aime encore,
Rendez-moi l'âge des amours;
Au crépuscule de mes jours
Rejoignez, s'il se peut, l'aurore.

Des beaux lieux où le dieu du vin
Avec l'Amour tient son empire,
Le Temps, qui me prend par la main,
M'avertit que je me retire.

De son inflexible rigueur
Tirons au moins quelque avantage.
Qui n'a pas l'esprit de son âge
De son âge a tout le malheur.

Laissons à la belle jeunesse
Ses folâtres emportements:
Nous ne vivons que deux moments;
Qu'il en soit un pour la sagesse.

Quoi! pour toujours vous me fuyez,
Tendresse, illusion, folie,
Dons du ciel, qui me consoliez
Des amertumes de la vie!

On meurt deux fois, je le vois bien:
Cesser d'aimer et d'être aimable,
C'est une mort insupportable;
Cesser de vivre, ce n'est rien.

Thus did I mourn to see depart
The all-too-pleasing dreams of youth,
And craved with fondly feeble heart
The bubbles sold in Folly's booth.

But clad in a serener splendor
Fond Friendship came from heaven above,
And proved perhaps more truly tender
Though not so bitter-sweet as love.

I gave my heart into her keeping—
Her charm was new, her worth was known:
I followed her, but followed weeping,
Because I followed her alone.

Translated by WILLIAM FREDERIC GIESE

While poetry may no longer be the greatest claim to renown of François-Marie Arouet (1694-1778), who took the name of Voltaire, some of his occasional poems are still of interest.

Madame du Châtelet is the intelligent and cultured lady at whose home Voltaire lived for about ten years after his return from exile in England. The poem to Madame du Châtelet was written when Voltaire was forty-seven. His Adieux à la Vie was written shortly before his death in 1778.

Ainsi je déplorais la perte
Des erreurs de mes premiers ans;
Et mon âme, aux désirs ouverte,
Regrettait ses égarements.

Du ciel alors daignant descendre,
L'amitié vint à mon secours;
Elle était peut-être aussi tendre,
Mais moins vive que les Amours.

Touché de sa beauté nouvelle,
Et de sa lumière éclairé,
Je la suivis; mais je pleurai
De ne pouvoir plus suivre qu'elle.

To Life, Farewell

Adieu. I'm going to that land
Whence returned not my dead father.
Forever adieu, my good friends,
You who will miss me scarce at all.
And you, my enemies, will laugh.
'Tis the usual requiem.
But you will taste of it one day;
And when, on those shadowy shores,
You go to reap your own reward,
Your passing will bring laughter, too.
        When on the stage of this planet
Each man has played his little rôle,
His turn having come to exit,
He is led offstage on signal.
In their bout with final illness
I have seen men of all degrees,
Old bishops and old magistrates,
Old courtesans in death's last pang:
Vainly in churchly panoply
Would come on scene with little bell
Equipage of the sacristy:
Vainly would priest anoint with oil
That dear old soul whose life was spent;
The scornful crowd made fun of him.
Satire for a moment did speak
Of the foolish acts of his life;
Then forever was he forgot;
And so at last the farce was done.
Purgatory or nothingness
Put an end to this comedy.

Adieux à la Vie

Adieu; je vais dans ce pays
D'où ne revint point feu mon père.
Pour jamais adieu, mes amis,
Qui ne me regretterez guère.
Vous en rirez, mes ennemis;
C'est le *requiem* ordinaire.
Vous en tâterez quelque jour;
Et lorsqu'aux ténébreux rivages
Vous irez trouver vos ouvrages,
Vous ferez rire à votre tour.
　　　　Quand sur la scène de ce monde
Chaque homme a joué son rôlet,
En partant il est à la ronde
Reconduit à coups de sifflet.
Dans leur dernière maladie
J'ai vu des gens de tous états,
Vieux évêques, vieux magistrats,
Vieux courtisans à l'agonie:
Vainement en cérémonie
Avec sa clochette arrivait
L'attirail de la sacristie;
Le curé vainement oignait
Notre vieille âme à sa sortie;
Le public malin s'en moquait;
La satire un moment parlait
Des ridicules de sa vie;
Puis à jamais on l'oubliait;
Ainsi la farce était finie.
Le purgatoire ou le néant
Terminait cette comédie.

Little butterflies of a day,
Invisible marionettes
That fly so rapidly in time
From Polichinelle to the tomb,
Tell me verily what you are.
At life's end, which I now come near,
What mortal needs least our pity?
He it is who can nothing fear,
Who lives and dies to fame unknown.

Translated by K. F. C.

Petits papillons d'un moment,
Invisibles marionnettes,
Qui volez si rapidement
De Polichinelle au néant,
Dites-moi donc ce que vous êtes.
Au terme où je suis parvenu,
Quel mortel est le moins à plaindre?
— C'est celui qui ne sait rien craindre,
Qui vit et qui meurt inconnu.

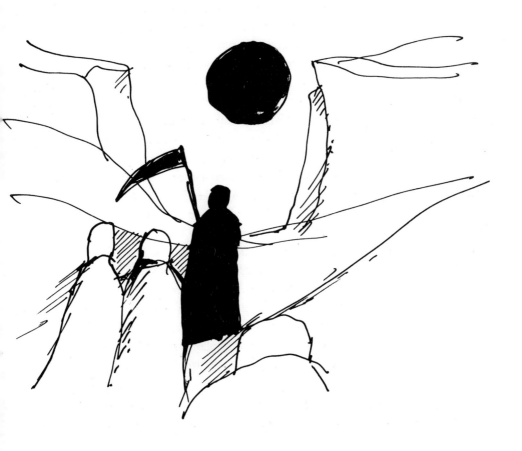

The Cricket

A poor lone little cricket
Hiding in a field in bloom
Was watching a butterfly
Flit about in the meadow.
The wingéd insect shone with the brightest colors,
Azure, crimson, and gold burst forth upon its wings;
Young, handsome, vain, it flies from flower to flower,
Choosing, then forsaking them all.
"Ah!" said the cricket, "how different are his fate
And mine own one; old Dame Nature
Granted all to him, to me not a single thing.
No talent have I, and surely not a figure;
No one pays heed to me, I am unseen down here;
I might as well be dead withal."
As he was talking, in the field
There arrives a group of children:
Right away there they are running
After that butterfly they all long for so much.
Hats, handkerchiefs, bonnets, all serve to ensnare it.
The poor insect searches vainly to escape them.
And soon it becomes their conquest.
One seizes its wing, another its small body.
A third child approaches and takes it by the head.
Scarce so much effort was needed
To tear the poor beast to pieces.
"Alas," said the cricket, "I'm no longer angry;
The price is far too steep to shine in this old world.
How content I shall be in my obscure retreat!
To live happy, let's live hidden."

Translated by K. F. C.

Jean-Pierre Claris de Florian (1755-1794) was a grand-nephew of Voltaire. He is remembered chiefly today for his fables, but he did write other poetry, as well as novels and plays.

Le Grillon

Un pauvre petit grillon,
Caché dans l'herbe fleurie,
Regardait un papillon
Voltigeant dans la prairie.
L'insecte ailé brillait des plus vives couleurs,
L'azur, le pourpre et l'or éclataient sur ses ailes;
Jeune, beau, petit-maître, il court de fleurs en fleurs,
Prenant et quittant les plus belles.
« Ah! disait le grillon, que son sort et le mien
Sont différents! Dame nature
Pour lui fit tout, et pour moi rien.
Je n'ai point de talent, encor moins de figure;
Nul ne prend garde à moi, l'on m'ignore ici-bas;
Autant vaudrait n'exister pas.»
Comme il parlait, dans la prairie,
Arrive une troupe d'enfants:
Aussitôt les voilà courants
Après ce papillon dont ils ont tous envie.
Chapeaux, mouchoirs, bonnets, servent à l'attraper.
L'insecte vainement cherche à leur échapper.
Il devient bientôt leur conquête.
L'un le saisit par l'aile, un autre par le corps;
Un troisième survient, et le prend par la tête.
Il ne fallait pas tant d'efforts
Pour déchirer la pauvre bête.
« Oh! Oh! dit le grillon, je ne suis plus fâché;
Il en coûte trop cher pour briller dans le monde.
Combien je vais aimer ma retraite profonde!
Pour vivre heureux, vivons caché.»

The Flute

When I remember I am nigh to weep:
How he would hold the flute unto my lip,
And, smiling, set me level with his heart,
Swearing I beat him at his own smooth art.
'Twas he who taught my faltering lip to draw
Sweet breath unbrokenly and without flaw
Of suavest melody; my hands unskilled
By his deft hands over the stops were drilled;
'Twas thus I learnt, though still with blundering heed,
To close the gaps upon the sounding reed.

Translated by WILFRID THORLEY

The eighteenth century in France was the age of reason and had little feeling for poetry. But toward the end it did produce one great poet, André Chénier (1762-1794). While Chénier was a good technician, his great love was for beauty, both visual and musical. He was a kind of Ronsard of the late eighteenth century who inspired a rebirth of poetry in France and whose influence on Vigny, Hugo, and Musset is marked. Chénier was actively sympathetic toward the French Revolution, but ironically, because he could not share in its excesses, he was guillotined at the age of thirty-one, just two days before the fall of Robespierre.

ANDRÉ CHÉNIER

Épigramme—La Leçon de Flûte

Toujours ce souvenir m'attendrit et me touche,
Quand lui-même, appliquant la flûte sur ma bouche,
Riant et m'asseyant sur lui, près de son coeur,
M'appelait son rival et déjà son vainqueur.
Il façonnait ma lèvre inhabile et peu sûre
À souffler une haleine harmonieuse et pure;
Et ses savantes mains prenaient mes jeunes doigts,
Les levaient, les baissaient, recommençaient vingt fois,
Leur enseignant ainsi, quoique faibles encore,
A fermer tour à tour les trous du buis sonore.

The Roses of Sa'adi

I wanted this morning to bring you a gift of roses;
But I took so many in my wide belt,
The tightened knots could not contain them all,

And burst asunder. The roses taking wing
On the wind, were all blown out to sea,
Following the water, never to return;

The waves were red with them as if aflame.
This evening my dress bears their perfume still:
You may take from it now their fragrant souvenir.

Translated by BARBARA HOWES

Marceline Desbordes-Valmore (1786-1859) was singer, actress, and poet. Her love poems are the pure lyricism of a gifted writer who had little formal education. Her simplicity, sincerity, and delightful musicality were much appreciated by romantic and symbolist poets alike.

Les Roses de Saadi

J'ai voulu ce matin te rapporter des roses;
Mais j'en avais tant pris dans mes ceintures closes
Que les noeuds trop serrés n'ont pu les contenir.

Les noeuds ont éclaté. Les roses, envolées
Dans le vent, à la mer s'en sont toutes allées.
Elles ont suivi l'eau pour ne plus revenir.

La vague en a paru rouge et comme enflammée.
Ce soir, ma robe encore en est tout embaumée . . .
Respires-en sur moi l'odorant souvenir!

The Lake

Thus ever drawn toward far shores uncharted,
Into eternal darkness borne away,
May we not ever on Time's sea, unthwarted,
  Cast anchor for a day?

O lake! Now hardly by a year grown older,
And nigh the well-known waves her eyes should greet,
Behold! I sit alone on this same boulder
  Thou knewest for her seat.

Thus didst thou murmur in thy rocky haven,
Thus didst thou shatter on its stony breast;
Thus fell the wind-flung foam on sands engraven
  Where her dear feet had prest.

One eve—rememberest thou?—in silence drifting,
'Twixt deep and sky no sound had echo save
Afar the rowers dipping oars and lifting
  Over thy waters suave.

When all at once a voice that made earth wonder
From the charmed shore drove all the echoes wide,
And rapt the wave, not fain as I nor fonder,
  And with sweet words did chide:

"Stay thou thy flight, O Time! and happy hours
  Trail by laggard feet!
Let all the savour of your delight be ours,
  Of all our days most sweet!

Le Lac

Ainsi, toujours poussés vers de nouveaux rivages,
Dans la nuit éternelle emportés sans retour,
Ne pourrons-nous jamais sur l'océan des âges
        Jeter l'ancre un seul jour?

O lac! l'année à peine a fini sa carrière,
Et près des flots chéris qu'elle devait revoir,
Regarde! je viens seul m'asseoir sur cette pierre
        Où tu la vis s'asseoir!

Tu mugissais ainsi sous ces roches profondes;
Ainsi tu te brisais sur leurs flancs déchirés;
Ainsi le vent jetait l'écume de tes ondes
        Sur ses pieds adorés.

Un soir, t'en souvient-il? nous voguions en silence,
On n'entendait au loin, sur l'onde et sous les cieux,
Que le bruit des rameurs qui frappaient en cadence
        Tes flots harmonieux.

Tout à coup des accents inconnus à la terre
Du rivage charmé frappèrent les échos;
Le flot fut attentif, et la voix qui m'est chère
        Laissa tomber ces mots:

« O temps, suspends ton vol! et vous, heures propices,
        Suspendez votre cours!
Laissez-nous savourer les rapides délices
        Des plus beaux de nos jours!

"Too many grieving souls to thee are praying;
      Nay, leave not these immune;
Bear off with thee their sorrows undelaying;
      Leave happy souls their boon.

"Nay, but in vain I ask one gracious hour;
      Time flies and will not hark.
I bid the night abide and dawn doth shower
      His splendour down the dark.

"Ah, let us love, my Love, for Time is heartless,
      Be happy while you may!
Man hath no Heaven and Time's coast is chartless.
      He speeds; we pass away!"

Churl Time, and can it be sweet moments cherished,
Wherein love fills our lives with teeming bliss,
Speed far away and be as swiftly perished
      As days when sorrow is?

Nay! Ere we go may we not leave sure traces?
Nay! Passed for ever? Beyond all reprieve?
What Time bestows on us, what Time effaces
      He nevermore shall give?

O! everlasting night, deep pit unsounded,
What dost thou with engulphéd days untold?
Speak! Wilt thou yield us back the bliss unbounded
      Once ravished from our hold?

O! lake, mute rocks, caves, leafy woodland shading,
You whom Time spares or clothes with newer sheen,
Keep of this night, fair Nature, keep unfading
      The memory ever green!

« Assez de malheureux ici-bas vous implorent:
Coulez, coulez pour eux;
Prenez avec leurs jours les soins qui les dévorent;
Oubliez les heureux.

« Mais je demande en vain quelques moments encore,
Le temps m'échappe et fuit;
Je dis à cette nuit: Sois plus lente; et l'aurore
Va dissiper la nuit.

« Aimons donc, aimons donc! de l'heure fugitive,
Hâtons-nous, jouissons!
L'homme n'a point de port, le temps n'a point de rive;
Il coule, et nous passons!»

Temps jaloux, se peut-il que ces moments d'ivresse,
Où l'amour à longs flots nous verse le bonheur,
S'envolent loin de nous de la même vitesse
Que les jours de malheur?

Eh quoi! n'en pourrons-nous fixer au moins la trace?
Quoi! Passés pour jamais? quoi! tout entiers perdus?
Ce temps qui les donna, ce temps qui les efface,
Ne nous les rendra plus?

Éternité, néant, passé, sombres abîmes,
Que faites-vous des jours que vous engloutissez?
Parlez: nous rendrez-vous ces extases sublimes
Que vous nous ravissez?

O lac! rochers muets! grottes! forêt obscure!
Vous que le temps épargne ou qu'il peut rajeunir,
Gardez de cette nuit, gardez, belle nature,
Au moins le souvenir!

In all thy calms and all thy tempests blending,
Fair lake, and in thy forelands' smiling fronts,
In thy dark pines and thy wild cliffs impending
    Over thy crystal fonts,

In the winds passing, with a trembling lightness,
Heard in the echoes that thy shores throw far,
Seen in the beams that fall with sheeny whiteness
    Wave-borne from the clear star!

Let moaning breezes thro' the rushes gliding,
All perfume stirring thy sweet air above,
All seen or heard or breathed bear this tiding,
    "Hereby they once did love!"

Translated by WILFRID THORLEY

Alphonse de Lamartine (1790-1869) is the first great French poet of the nineteenth century. His early poetry is his best and is extremely personal. All the emotions are there, hope and despair, fond memories and regret for times past, frustration at the rapid flight of time, profound questions concerning destiny and death, and hope for eternal life. These feelings are allied to a love of nature to which the poet calls for solace.

Lamartine also had an important career as diplomat and politician, becoming head of the provisional government after the Revolution of 1848 only to be roundly defeated for the presidency of the Republic in December of the same year by Prince Louis-Napoleon.

Qu'il soit dans ton repos, qu'il soit dans tes orages,
Beau lac, et dans l'aspect de tes riants coteaux,
Et dans ces noirs sapins, et dans ces rocs sauvages
    Qui pendent sur tes eaux!

Qu'il soit dans le zéphyr qui frémit et qui passe,
Dans les bruits de tes bords par tes bords répétés,
Dans l'astre au front d'argent qui blanchit ta surface
    De ses molles clartés!

Que le vent qui gémit, le roseau qui soupire,
Que les parfums légers de ton air embaumé,
Que tout ce qu'on entend, l'on voit ou l'on respire,
    Tout dise: « Ils ont aimé! »

The Horn

I

I love the call of horns from woods at night,
When sounding terror to some doe in flight,
Or the last notes of the huntsman's echoing song
That trembling wind-stirred leaves faintly prolong.

How oft at midnight it has reached my ears,
To wake my lonely smiles, more oft my tears!
It seemed to me prophetic song that told
Impending death to paladins of old.

Loved mountain, azure in the sparkling day!
Frazona! high ringed rocks of Marboré!
O snow-fed falls that murmur in my dreams!
Ye Pyrenean springs, cascades and streams!

O flowered slopes, great Throne where seasons meet,
With brow of ice, and green sward at thy feet!
'Tis there, 'tis there the distant horn may be
Best heard to sigh its tender elegy.

'Tis there lone travellers oft the darkness fill
With brazen echoes when the air is still;
That measured music blends there on the fell
With tuneful tinkling from the young lamb's bell.

In full view hangs a doe upon a rock
And listens motionless with ears acock,
While in the falls' eternal vast lament
The ancient epics of Romance are blent.

Le Cor

I

J'aime le son du cor, le soir, au fond des bois,
Soit qu'il chante les pleurs de la biche aux abois,
Ou l'adieu du chasseur que l'écho faible accueille
Et que le vent du nord porte de feuille en feuille.

Que de fois, seul, dans l'ombre à minuit demeuré,
J'ai souri de l'entendre, et plus souvent pleuré!
Car je croyais ouïr de ces bruits prophétiques
Qui précédaient la mort des paladins antiques.

O montagnes d'azur! ô pays adoré,
Rocs de la Frazona, cirque du Marboré,
Cascades qui tombez des neiges entraînées,
Sources, gaves, ruisseaux, torrents des Pyrénées;

Monts gelés et fleuris, trônes des deux saisons,
Dont le front est de glace et le pied de gazons!
C'est là qu'il faut s'asseoir, c'est là qu'il faut entendre
Les airs lointains d'un cor mélancolique et tendre.

Souvent un voyageur, lorsque l'air est sans bruit,
De cette voix d'airain fait retentir la nuit;
À ses chants cadencés autour de lui se mêle
L'harmonieux grelot du jeune agneau qui bêle.

Une biche attentive, au lieu de se cacher,
Se suspend immobile au sommet du rocher,
Et la cascade unit, dans une chute immense,
Son éternelle plainte aux chants de la romance.

Souls of old Knights, are ye abroad once more?
Is't ye whom in the horn's far song I hear?
Roncevaux! athwart thy valley, desolate,
Great Roland's shade still roams, disconsolate.

II

He stands alone, though not a Knight has fled.
Hard by lies Oliver: the rest are dead.
Upon the peak still quakes the Afric host.
"Yield, Roland," cries the Moor, "or you are lost.

"In torrent-beds your stricken peers all lie."
With tiger's rage he roareth, "Yield will I,
O Moor, when summits of the Pyrenees
Roll past me on these waters to the seas."

"Yield then or die, for here they are: behold!"
And bound, hurtling from the top peak, rolled
A huge rock, breaking pines on the mountainside
And crashing in th' abyss. Then Roland cried

"Thanks for this path." And with one hand he swept
It to the mountain foot and giant-like leapt
Upon the buttressed rock; and at this sight
The wavering host prepared to take to flight.

III

Meanwhile Charlemagne and all his knights, care-free,
Descend the mountain, talking cheerily.
With waters shining on the skyline, lo,
The vales of Luz and Argèles gleam below.

Âmes des chevaliers, revenez-vous encor?
Est-ce vous qui parlez avec la voix du cor?
Roncevaux! Roncevaux! dans ta sombre vallée
L'ombre du grand Roland n'est donc pas consolée?

II

Tous les preux étaient morts, mais aucun n'avait fui.
Il reste seul debout, Olivier près de lui;
L'Afrique sur le mont l'entoure et tremble encore.
« Roland, tu vas mourir, rends-toi, criait le More;

« Tous tes pairs sont couchés dans les eaux des torrents.»
Il rugit comme un tigre et dit: « Si je me rends,
Africain, ce sera lorsque les Pyrénées
Sur l'onde avec leurs corps rouleront entraînées.

— Rends-toi donc, répond-il, ou meurs, car les voilà;»
Et du plus haut des monts un grand rocher roula.
Il bondit, il roula jusqu'au fond de l'abîme,
Et de ces pins, dans l'onde, il vint briser la cime.

« Merci! cria Roland; tu m'as fait un chemin.»
Et, jusqu'au pied des monts le roulant d'une main,
Sur le roc affermi comme un géant s'élance;
Et, prête à fuir, l'armée à ce seul pas balance.

III

Tranquilles cependant, Charlemagne et ses preux
Descendaient la montagne et se parlaient entre eux.
À l'horizon déjà, par leurs eaux signalées,
De Luz et d'Argelès se montraient les vallées.

The troops applaud, for now the troubadour
Tunes his lute for "The Willows of Adour."
In alien goblets wine flows from French presses,
And laughing soldiers talk to shepherdesses.

For Roland holds the heights; why be afraid?
As Turpin rode his palfrey all arrayed
In purple, with the relics in his hand,
He burst out as the burning heavens he scanned:

"Behold the sky aflame with clouds of fire!
Ah, tempt not God, but call a halt, O Sire,
For, by Saint Denis, those be souls that ride
Through Heaven on yon blazing mist astride!

"Twice did the lightning flash, then twice again!"
And now, afar, they hear the Horn's faint strain.—
The Emperor, perturbed, holds back in fear
And checks his charger's overbold career.

"You hear?" says he. —"Yes, 'tis the shepherd wights
That call their scattered flocks back from the heights,"
The Bishop says, "or haply it may have been
King Oberon who called his Faery Queen."

Charlemagne speeds on, his brow blacker with care
Than Thunderclouds that shroud the menaced air.
—Has Roland been betrayed? . . . Forth wells the Horn!
It dies; begins afresh, — prolonged, — forlorn!

"Alas! my nephew! for if Roland cries
For succour, then 'tis certain that he dies!
Back, Knights! The mountain must be crossed again!
Quake at our tread once more, false soil of Spain!"

L'armée applaudissait. Le luth du troubadour
S'accordait pour chanter les saules de l'Adour;
Le vin français coulait dans la coupe étrangère;
Le soldat, en riant, parlait à la bergère.

Roland gardait les monts: tous passaient san effroi.
Assis nonchalamment sur un noir palefroi
Qui marchait revêtu de housses violettes,
Turpin disait, tenant les saintes amulettes:

« Sire, on voit dans le ciel des nuages de feu;
Suspendez votre marche; il ne faut tenter Dieu.
Par monsieur saint Denis! certes ce sont des âmes
Qui passent dans les airs sur ces vapeurs de flammes.

« Deux éclairs ont relui, puis deux autres encor.»
Ici l'on entendait le son lointain du cor.
L'empereur étonné, se jetant en arrière,
Suspend du destrier la marche aventurière.

« Entendez-vous? dit-il. — Oui, ce sont des pasteurs
Rappelant les troupeaux épars sur les hauteurs,
Répondit l'archevêque, ou la voix étouffée
Du nain vert Obéron, qui parle avec sa fée.»

Et l'empereur poursuit; mais son front soucieux
Est plus sombre et plus noir que l'orage des cieux;
Il craint la trahison, et, tandis qu'il y songe,
Le cor éclate et meurt, renaît et se prolonge.

« Malheur! c'est mon neveu! malheur! car, si Roland
Appelle â son secours, ce doit être en mourant.
Arrière, chevaliers, repassons la montagne!
Tremble encor sous nos pieds, sol trompeur de l'Espagne!»

Upon a crest the steeds halt, white and foaming:
Below is Roncevaux, ashen in the gloaming,
Amid the evening's pale and burnt-out light.
Afar the Moorish flag is seen in flight.

"What see'st Thou, Turpin, in torrent bed?"
—"I see two Knights, one dying and one dead.
Crushed beneath a huge black rock they lie;
The stronger holds an ivory Horn on high!
His soul, expiring, called us twice, forlorn."

Ah, God! how sad from deep woods sounds the horn!

Translated by ALAN CONDER

Alfred de Vigny (1797-1863)—Son of an army officer, Vigny followed in his father's footsteps, but found little glory in the profession. During the Spanish campaign in 1823 Vigny got no farther than a barracks in Pau where military monotony drove him to literature. It was during his stay at Pau, in the Pyrenees, that he was inspired to write Le Cor, *his long poem describing the episode of* La Chanson de Roland *in which Roland, Charlemagne's nephew, lost his life at the hands of the Saracens. Honor, stoicism, and self-denial, three outstanding ideals of Vigny, are strikingly represented in the poem.*

IV

Sur le plus haut des monts s'arrêtent les chevaux;
L'écume les blanchit; sous leurs pieds, Roncevaux
Des feux mourants du jour à peine se colore.
À l'horizon lointain fuit l'étendard du More.

« Turpin, tu n'as rien vu dans le fond torrent?
— J'y vois deux chevaliers: l'un mort, l'autre expirant.
Tous deux sont écrasés sous une roche noire;
Le plus fort, dans sa main, élève un cor d'ivoire,
Son âme en s'exhalant nous appela deux fois.»

Dieu! que le son du cor est triste au fond des bois!

Ecstasy

I stood by the waves, while the stars soared in sight,
Not a cloud specked the sky, not a sail shimmered bright;
Scenes beyond this dim world were revealed to mine eye;
And the woods, and the hills, and all nature around,
Seemed to question with moody, mysterious sound,
   The waves, and the pure stars on high.

And the clear constellations, that infinite throng,
While thousand rich harmonies swelled in their song,
Replying, bowed meekly their diamond-blaze—
And the blue waves, which nothing may bind or arrest,
Chorused forth, as they stooped the white foam of their crest:
   "Creator! We bless thee and praise!"

Translated by R. C. ELLWOOD

Victor Hugo (1802-1885)—is poet, novelist, dramatist, leader of the Romantic movement, politician, and statesman. In all of these he was a dynamo of creativity. At age fifteen he was already honored by the French Academy. At twenty-five he had written the Preface to Cromwell, *outlining the principles of Romantic drama. A liberal in literature and in politics, Hugo opposed Napoleon III and went into exile in 1851, not to return to Paris until 1870. By the completeness and profusion of his poetic genius Victor Hugo dominates the nineteenth century in France.*

Extase

Et j'entendis une grande voix.   *Apocalypse.*

J'étais seul près des flots, par une nuit d'étoiles.
Pas un nuage aux cieux, sur les mers pas de voiles.
Mes yeux plongeaient plus loin que le monde réel.
Et les bois, et les monts, et toute la nature,
Semblaient interroger dans un confus murmure
       Les flots des mers, les feux du ciel.

Et les étoiles d'or, légions infinies,
À voix haute, à voix basse, avec mille harmonies,
Disaient, en inclinant leurs couronnes de feu;
Et les flots bleus, que rien ne gouverne et n'arrête,
Disaient, en recourbant l'écume de leur crête:
       — C'est le Seigneur, le Seigneur Dieu!

The Sower

Now falls the dusk. I sit in peace
Beneath this gateway and behold
The ebbing daylight bring release
From toil by wood and wold.

With stirring at my heart I heed
Above the furrows night has steeped
A ragged sower throwing seed
Of harvests still unreaped.

His tall black silhouette above
The tillage strides on. How brave
Must be his faith that time will move
The grain within its grave.

He crosses the unending plain,
Now back, now forth; with open palm
He flings it wide and fills again,
While here I muse in calm;

And his vast shadow from below
Uplifted like a sail unfurled
With mighty rumour seems to sow
Athwart the starry world.

Translated by WILFRID THORLEY

VICTOR HUGO

Saison des Semailles

C'est le moment crépusculaire.
J'admire, assis sous un portail,
Ce reste de jour dont s'éclaire
La dernière heure du travail.

Dans les terres, de nuit baignées,
Je contemple, ému, les haillons
D'un vieillard qui jette à poignées
La moisson future aux sillons.

Sa haute silhouette noire
Domine les profonds labours.
On sent à quel point il doit croire
À la fuite utile des jours.

Il marche dans la plaine immense,
Va, vient, lance la graine au loin,
Rouvre sa main et recommence,
Et je médite, obscur témoin,

Pendant que, déployant ses voiles,
L'ombre, où se mêle une rumeur,
Semble élargir jusqu'aux étoiles
Le geste auguste du semeur.

The Djinns

Et come i gru van cantando lor lai
Facendo in aer di se lunga riga,
Cosi vid' io venir, traendo guai,
Ombre portate dalla detta briga. — DANTE

And like cranes that wing through the air in long files, singing their complaint, so saw I great gray clouds coming, borne by the storm, with weird wailing and moaning trailing in their wake.

Town, tower,
Shore, deep,
Where lower
Cliffs steep;
Waves gray,
Where play
Winds gay,
All asleep.

Hark! a sound,
Far and slight,
Breathes around
On the night:
High and higher,
Nigh and nigher,
Like a fire,
Roaring, bright.

Les Djinns

Et come i gru van cantando lor lai
Facendo in aer di se lunga riga,
Cosi vid' io venir, traendo guai,
Ombre portate dalla detta briga. — DANTE

Et comme les grues qui font dans l'air de longues files vont chantant leur plainte,
ainsi je vis venir traînant des gémissements des ombres emportées par cette tempête.

Murs, ville,
Et port,
Asile
De mort,
Mer grise
Où brise
La brise,
Tout dort.

Dans la plaine
Naît un bruit.
C'est l'haleine
De la nuit.
Elle brame
Comme une âme
Qu'une flamme
Toujours suit.

Now, on 'tis sweeping
With rattling beat,
Like dwarf imp leaping
In gallop fleet:
He flies, he prances,
In frolic fancies,
On wave-crest dances
With pattering feet.

Hark, the rising swell,
With each new burst!
Like the tolling bell
Of a convent curst;
Like the billowy roar
On a storm-lashed shore,—
Now hushed, but once more
Maddening to its worst.

O God! the deadly sound
Of the Djinn's fearful cry!
Quick, 'neath the spiral round
Of the deep staircase fly!
See, see our lamplight fade!
And of the balustrade
Mounts, mounts the circling shade
Up to the ceiling high!

'Tis the Djinn's wild streaming swarm
Whistling in their tempest flight;
Snap the tall yews 'neath the storm,
Like a pine flame crackling bright.
Swift, though heavy, lo! their crowd
Through the heavens rushing loud
Like a livid thunder-cloud
With its bolt of fiery might!

La voix plus haute
Semble un grelot.
D'un nain qui saute
C'est le galop.
Il fuit, s'élance,
Puis en cadence
Sur un pied danse
Au bout d'un flot.

La rumeur approche,
L'écho la redit.
C'est comme la cloche
D'un couvent maudit,
Comme un bruit de foule
Qui tonne et qui roule,
Et tantôt s'écroule,
Et tantôt grandit.

Dieu! la voix sépulcrale
Des Djinns! Quel bruit ils font!
Fuyons sous la spirale
De l'escalier profond!
Déjà s'éteint ma lampe,
Et l'ombre de la rampe,
Qui le long du mur rampe,
Monte jusqu'au plafond.

C'est l'essaim des Djinns qui passe
Et tourbillonne en sifflant.
Les ifs, que leur vol fracasse,
Craquent comme un pin brûlant.
Leur troupeau lourd et rapide,
Volant dans l'espace vide,
Semble un nuage livide
Qui porte un éclair au flanc.

Ho! they are on us, close without!
Shut tight the shelter where we lie!
With hideous din the monster rout,
Dragon and vampire, fill the sky!
The loosened rafter overhead
Trembles and bends like quivering reed;
Shakes the old door with shuddering dread,
As from its rusty hinge 'twould fly!

Wild cries of hell! voices that howl and shriek!
The horrid troop before the tempest tossed—
O Heaven!—descends my lowly roof to seek:
Bends the strong wall beneath the furious host.
Totters the house as though, like dry leaf shorn
From autumn bough and on the mad blast borne,
Up from its deep foundations it were torn
To join the stormy whirl. Ah! all is lost!

O Prophet! if thy hand but now
Save from these hellish things,
A pilgrim at thy shrine I'll bow,
Laden with pious offerings.
Bid their hot breath its fiery rain
Stream on the faithful's door in vain;
Vainly upon my blackened pane
Grate the fierce claws of their dark wings!

They have passed!—and their wild legion
Cease to thunder at my door;
Fleeting through night's rayless region,
Hither they return no more.
Clanking chains and sounds of woe
Fill the forests as they go;
And the tall oaks cower low,
Bent their flaming light before.

Ils sont tout près! — Tenons fermée
Cette salle où nous les narguons.
Quel bruit dehors! Hideuse armée
De vampires et de dragons!
La poutre du toit descellée
Ploie ainsi qu'une herbe mouillée,
Et la vieille porte rouillée
Tremble à déraciner ses gonds.

Cris de l'enfer! voix qui hurle et qui pleure!
L'horrible essaim, poussé par l'aquilon,
Sans doute, ô ciel! s'abat sur ma demeure.
Le mur fléchit sous le noir bataillon.
La maison crie et chancelle penchée,
Et l'on dirait que, du sol arrachée,
Ainsi qu'il chasse une feuille séchée,
Le vent la roule avec leur tourbillon!

Prophète! si ta main me sauve
De ces impurs démons des soirs,
J'irai prosterner mon front chauve
Devant tes sacrés encensoirs!
Fais que sur ces portes fidèles
Meure leur souffle d'étincelles,
Et qu'en vain l'ongle de leurs ailes
Grince et crie à ces vitraux noirs!

Ils sont passés! — Leur cohorte
S'envole et fuit, et leurs pieds
Cessent de battre ma porte
De leurs coups multipliés.
L'air est plein d'un bruit de chaînes,
Et dans les forêts prochaines
Frissonnent tous les grands chênes,
Sous leur vol de feu pliés!

On! on! the storm of wings
Bears far the fiery fear,
Till scarce the breeze now brings
Dim murmurings to the ear;
Like locusts' humming hail,
Or thrash of tiny flail
Plied by the fitful gale
On some old roof-tree sere.

Fainter now are borne
Feeble mutterings still;
As when Arab horn
Swells its magic peal,
Shoreward o'er the deep
Fairy voices sweep,
And the infant's sleep
Golden visions fill.

Each deadly Djinn,
Dark child of fright,
Of death and sin,
Speeds in wild flight.
Hark, the dull moan,
Like the deep tone
Of Ocean's groan
Afar, by night!

More and more
Fades it slow,
As on shore
Ripples flow,—
As the plaint
Far and faint
Of a saint
Murmured low.

De leurs ailes lointaines
Le battement décroît,
Si confus dans les plaines,
Si faible, que l'on croit
Ouïr la sauterelle
Crier d'une voix grêle
Ou pétiller la grêle
Sur le plomb d'un vieux toit.

D'étranges syllabes
Nous viennent encor;
Ainsi, des arabes
Quand sonne le cor,
Un chant sur la grève
Par instants s'élève,
Et l'enfant qui rêve
Fait des rêves d'or.

Les Djinns funèbres,
Fils du trépas,
Dans les ténèbres
Pressent leur pas;
Leur essaim gronde:
Ainsi, profonde,
Murmure une onde
Qu'on ne voit pas.

Ce bruit vague
Qui s'endort,
C'est la vague
Sur le bord;
C'est la plainte
Presque éteinte
D'une sainte
Pour un mort.

Hark! hist!
Around,
I list!
The bounds
Of space
All trace
Efface
Of sound.

Translated by JOHN L. O'SULLIVAN

On doute
La nuit . . .
J'écoute: —
Tout fuit.
Tout passe;
L'espace
Efface
Le bruit.

Sadness

My little life I've lived in vain,
Friendship has fled and gaiety,
And pride can never bloom again
That once the Muses woke in me.

When Truth unveiled her shining face,
I thought to find in her a friend;
But day by day she lost her grace,
I grew to hate her in the end.

Yet Truth is an immortal Thing,
And none without her tutoring
In the world's way can be adept.

Truth is God's voice; I must respond,
Even though I find no joy beyond
This one—that I have sometimes wept.

Translated by WILLIAM FREDERIC GIESE

Alfred de Musset (1810-1847) was a brilliant student who early tried law, medicine, music, and art only to find that literature was his true vocation. By the age of nineteen he had become the spoiled prodigy of a group of Romantic writers headed by Victor Hugo and had written his Contes d'Espagne et d'Italie *in an extreme Romantic style. But Musset was destined to become an independent whose natural taste turned toward classicism. His thought and writing were also deeply affected by his brief and painful liaison with George Sand. Fantasy, tenderness, and intense personal suffering are characteristic of his work.*

Tristesse

J'ai perdu ma force et ma vie,
Et mes amis et ma gaîté;
J'ai perdu jusqu'à la fierté
Qui faisait croire à mon génie.

Quand j'ai connu la Vérité,
J'ai cru que c'était une amie;
Quand je l'ai comprise et sentie,
J'en étais déjà dégoûté.

Et pourtant elle est éternelle,
Et ceux qui se sont passés d'elle
Ici-bas ont tout ignoré.

Dieu parle, il faut qu'on lui réponde;
Le seul bien qui me reste au monde
Est d'avoir quelquefois pleuré.

Mimi Pinson
Song

Mimi Pinson has fair tresses;
Everyone knows Mimi.
In a world of many dresses,
   Only one has Mimi,
   Tra la, tra la,
And one bonnet.
The Grand Turk has many a one.
   This keeps her good—God's will is done,
Nobody can e'er put in pawn
That one dress of Mimi Pinson.

Mimi Pinson wears a white rose.
A white rose wears Mimi.
In her heart its petals unclose,
   In the heart of Mimi,
   Tra la, tra la,
Joy is abloom.
When good cheer her spirit raises,
   She sings out in joyous phrases.
Oft her ear has tilted on it,
Gaily, Mimi Pinson's bonnet.

Sawbones, watching those eyes so bright,
Quick hands, too, of Mimi,
Wear out their sleeves, both day and night,
   Leaning towards Mimi,
   Tra la, tra la,
On her counter.
Harming none, but lessons teaching,
   Sorbonne's learning far outreaching,
All rumpling, she has frowned upon,
Of the dress of Mimi Pinson.

Mimi Pinson

Chanson

Mimi Pinson est une blonde,
Une blonde que l'on connaît.
Elle n'a qu'une robe au monde,
     Landerirette!
      Et qu'un bonnet.
Le Grand Turc en a davantage.
Dieu voulut, de cette façon,
     La rendre sage.
On ne peut pas la mettre en gage,
La robe de Mimi Pinson.

Mimi Pinson porte une rose,
Une rose blanche au côté.
Cette fleur dans son coeur éclose,
     Landerirette!
      C'est la gaîté.
Quand un bon souper la réveille,
Elle fait sortir la chanson
     De la bouteille.
Parfois il penche sur l'oreille,
Le bonnet de Mimi Pinson.

Elle a les yeux et la main prestes.
Les carabins, matin et soir,
Usent les manches de leurs vestes,
     Landerirette!
      À son comptoir.
Quoique sans maltraiter personne,
Mimi leur fait mieux la leçon
     Qu'à la Sorbonne.
Il ne faut pas qu'on la chiffonne,
La robe de Mimi Pinson.

Mimi Pinson may never wed;
If God wills so, Mimi,
There is always sewing with thread
    And needle for Mimi,
    Tra la, tra la,
And her fingers.
Good looks without worth ne'er will win.
    In Mimi's heart a place within.
A cool head rests, depend on it,
Under Mimi Pinson's bonnet.

Should love with orange blossom grace
The bent head of Mimi,
She then will offer in its place
    Love's gift from Mimi,
    Tra la, tra la,
Her wedding gift.
No cloak 'tis, lined with ermine white,
    And borne on an escutcheon bright,
But, case for a pearl—guess not wrong—
'Tis the dress of Mimi Pinson.

While in her heart Republican,
Fine of soul is Mimi.
Three days waged she war like a man,
    In short gown of Mimi,
    Tra la, tra la,
Before their eyes.
For halberd, her bodkin wielding,
    Bold, she mounted guard unyielding.
Happy man whose cocade on it,
Flaunts on Mimi Pinson's bonnet.

Translated by JESSIE HENDRY McEWAN

Mimi Pinson peut rester fille;
Si Dieu le veut, c'est dans son droit.
Elle aura toujours son aiguille,
Landerirette!
Au bout du doigt.
Pour entreprendre sa conquête,
Ce n'est pas tout qu'un beau garçon;
Faut être honnête.
Car il n'est pas loin de sa tête,
Le bonnet de Mimi Pinson.

D'un gros bouquet de fleurs d'orange
Si l'amour veut la couronner,
Elle a quelque chose en échange,
Landerirette!
À lui donner.
Ce n'est pas, on se l'imagine,
Un manteau sur un écusson
Fourré d'hermine;
C'est l'étui d'une perle fine,
La robe de Mimi Pinson.

Mimi n'a pas l'âme vulgaire,
Mais son coeur est républicain.
Aux trois jours elle a fait la guerre,
Landerirette!
En casaquin.
A défaut d'une hallebarde,
On l'a vue avec son poinçon
Monter la garde.
Heureux qui mettra sa cocarde
Au bonnet de Mimi Pinson!

Epitaph

Now, like a starling's, all his life was gay—
Amorous, careless, tender—each in turn;
Now, a sad lover, dreamy ... taciturn ...
He heard a knocking at his door one day,

And it was Death! He asked his guest to stay
While his last sonnet found its final line,
Then calmly he arranged his body in
His icy coffin; shivering there he lay.

He was too lazy (so the tales implied);
Too often in his desk his ink-well dried.
All things he longed to know—but nothing knew.

And when he found his joy in life grow dim,
One winter night his soul was snatched from him ...
"Why did I come?" he asked—and so withdrew.

Translated by BRIAN HILL

Gérard de Nerval (Gérard Labrunie) (1808-1855) is important in French literature for the influence which his work is to have on the symbolists and surrealists. Nerval was attracted by German literature and translated Goethe's Faust *into French. Intermittently he was threatened by insanity. Nerval believed that dreams were of another world, a superior consciousness, another way of thinking in which his earthly life and memories were transformed. He attempted repeatedly to analyze these dreams which threatened his sanity.*

Épitaphe

Il a vécu, tantôt gai comme un sansonnet,
Tour à tour amoureux, insoucieux et tendre,
Tantôt sombre et rêveur, comme un triste Clitandre.
Un jour, il entendit qu'à sa porte on sonnait:

C'était la mort. Alors, il la pria d'attendre
Qu'il eût posé le point à son dernier sonnet;
Et puis, sans s'émouvoir, il s'en alla s'étendre
Au fond du coffre froid où son corps frissonnait.

Il était paresseux, à ce que dit l'histoire;
Il laissait trop sécher l'encre dans l'écritoire;
Il voulut tout savoir, mais il n'a rien connu;

Et quand vint le moment où, las de cette vie,
Un soir d'hiver, enfin, l'âme lui fut ravie,
Il s'en alla, disant: « Pourquoi suis-je venu? »

The Pot of Flowers

Sometimes a small boy finds a tiny seed
And takes a porcelain pot whose colours charm
His eye to serve it as a garden-bed,
Where monstrous blossoms and blue dragons swarm.

He goes away. Down snakes the coiling root;
The stem lifts from the soil, grows, branches out;
While deeper daily dives its hairy foot,
Until it bursts the belly of the pot.

The child comes back. He wonders much to see
Above the shards the stout green daggers dart;
The stalk is tough; he cannot tug it free;
Against the thorns his stubborn fingers smart.

So, in my wondering soul, is love begot:
A simple flower of Spring I thought I'd sown;
In coloured fragments lies the porcelain pot
Where a huge aloe's root went thrusting down!

Translated by BRIAN HILL

Théophile Gautier (1811-1872) advocated art for art's sake, which became the motto of the Parnassian group of poets. For Gautier art was to be beautiful, not useful. It had to be independent of politics and morality. Only beauty is eternal. Poetry should close ranks with the plastic arts. Beauty can be attained only by attention to every tiny detail. What is facile is to be avoided. The poet should adopt difficult meters, be careful in his choice of rhyme, explore the sounds of words, change visual images into musical impressions. Gautier's interest in painting made him very conscious of color and form.

Le Pot de Fleurs

Parfois un enfant trouve une petite graine,
Et tout d'abord, charmé de ses vives couleurs,
Pour la planter, il prend un pot de porcelaine
Orné de dragons bleus et de bizarres fleurs.

Il s'en va. La racine en couleuvres s'allonge,
Sort de terre, fleurit et devient arbrisseau;
Chaque jour, plus avant son pied chevelu plonge
Tant qu'il fasse éclater le ventre du vaisseau.

L'enfant revient; surpris, il voit la plante grasse
Sur les débris du pot brandir ses verts poignards;
Il la veut arracher, mais sa tige est tenace;
Il s'obstine, et ses doigt s'ensanglantent aux dards.

Ainsi germa l'amour dans mon âme surprise:
Je croyais ne semer qu'une fleur de printemps;
C'est un grand aloès dont la racine brise
Le pot de porcelaine aux dessins éclatants.

And with a tender dread
Upon an agate's face
> Retrace
Apollo's golden head.

Despise a watery hue
And tints that soon expire.
> With fire
Burn thine enamel true.

Twine, twine in artful wise
The blue-green mermaid's arms,
> Mid charms
Of thousand heraldries.

Show in their triple lobe
Virgin and Child, that hold
> Their globe,
Cross crowned and aureoled.

—All things return to dust
Save beauties fashioned well.
> The bust
Outlasts the citadel.

Oft doth the plowman's heel
Breaking an ancient clod,
> Reveal
A Caesar or a god.

The gods, too, die, alas!
But deathless and more strong
> Than brass
Remains the sovereign song.

D'une main délicate
Poursuis dans un filon
        D'agate
Le profil d'Apollon.

Peintre, fuis l'aquarelle,
Et fixe la couleur
        Trop frêle
Au four de l'émailleur.

Fais les sirènes bleues,
Tordant de cent façons
        Leurs queues,
Les monstres des blasons;

Dans son nimbe trilobe
La Vierge et son Jésus,
        Le globe
Avec la croix dessus.

Tout passe. — L'art robuste
Seul a l'éternité.
        Le buste
Survit à la cité.

Et la médaille austère
Que trouve un laboureur
        Sous terre
Révèle un empereur.

Les dieux eux-mêmes meurent.
Mais les vers souverains
        Demeurent
Plus forts que les airains.

Chisel and carve and file,
Till thy vague dream imprint
            Its smile
On thy unyielding flint.

Translated by GEORGE SANTAYANA

Sculpte, lime, cisèle;
Que ton rêve flottant
    Se scelle
Dans le bloc résistant!

Noël

The earth is white, and black the sky;—
Bells, sound your music gay and wild!—
Jesus is born. How tenderly
Mary's sweet face leans to her child.

No curtain is festooned within
To keep the baby from the cold;
Only the webs the spiders spin
Hang from the roof-beams fold on fold.

He shivers on the cold straw there,
The small dear Jesus, lowly laid;
But ox and ass draw gently near
And breathe to warm the manger bed.

Snow frames the thatched eaves of the byre;
On high the opening heavens fill,
As, robed in white, an angel choir
To shepherds chants, "Noël! Noël!"

Translated by BRIAN HILL

Noël

Le ciel est noir, la terre est blanche;
— Cloches, carillonnez gaîment! —
Jésus est né; — la Vierge penche
Sur lui son visage charmant.

Pas de courtines festonnées
Pour préserver l'enfant du froid;
Rien que les étoiles d'araignées
Qui pendent des poutres du toit.

Il tremble sur la paille fraîche,
Ce cher petit enfant Jésus,
Et pour l'échauffer dans sa crèche
L'âne et le boeuf soufflent dessus.

La neige au chaume coud ses franges,
Mais sur le toit s'ouvre le ciel
Et, tout en blanc, le choeur des anges
Chante aux bergers: « Noël! Noël! »

Tea

Miss Ellen, please pour me some tea
In the beautiful Chinese cup
Where goldfish seek to raise the ire
Of a pink and frightened monster.

I love the crazy cruelty
Of the chimeras that one tames;
Miss Ellen, please pour me some tea
In the beautiful Chinese cup.

There beneath an angry red sky
A proud lady full of cunning
Shows ecstasy and naïveté
In her long eyes of turquoise hue:
Miss Ellen, please pour me some tea.

Translated by K. F. C.

Théodore de Banville (1823-1891)—is a friend and disciple of Gautier. As a poet of the Parnassian group, Banville is a technician rather than a profound thinker. His overemphasis on rhyme to convey thought and feeling has been severely criticized.

Le Thé

Miss Ellen, versez-moi le Thé
Dans la belle tasse chinoise,
Où des poissons d'or cherchent noise
Au monstre rose épouvanté.

J'aime la folle cruauté
Des chimères qu'on apprivoise:
Miss Ellen, versez-moi le Thé
Dans la belle tasse chinoise.

Là sous un ciel rouge irrité,
Une dame fière et sournoise
Montre en ses longs yeux de turquoise
L'extase et la naïveté:
Miss Ellen, versez-moi le Thé.

The Elephants

A billowing sea of sand no eye can span
Lies sunk in flaming stillness in its bed.
Behind the copper skyline where the red
And misty dunes are shrouded, there dwells man.

No life, no sound. The full-gorged lions sleep
In hidden caves a hundred leagues away.
Beneath the date-trees, where the panthers prey,
Giraffes drink at the fountains blue and deep.

No bird that thick air cleaves with thrashing wing.
Warmed by a monstrous circling sun, a snake
Stirs sluggishly in sleep but does not wake;
His undulating back is glistening.

While thus with blazing air the heavens flame,
While sleep holds all that dismal solitude,
The ponderous elephants' slow and rugged brood
Across the desert marches towards its home.

Raising dust on the skyline, dark forms beat
The earth. They come, and, so that from the straight
And long-drawn line they shall not deviate,
They trample sand-dunes down with huge sure feet.

An old chief first with rude ridged body marches,
Hide like a gnawed tree ages undermine:
His head's a rock; the great bow of his spine
With every moment powerfully arches.

Les Éléphants

Le sable rouge est comme une mer sans limite,
Et qui flambe, muette, affaissée en son lit.
Une ondulation immobile remplit
L'horizon aux vapeurs de cuivre où l'homme habite.

Nulle vie et nul bruit. Tous les lions repus
Dorment au fond de l'antre éloigné de cent lieues,
Et la girafe boit dans les fontaines bleues,
Là-bas, sous les dattiers des panthères connus.

Pas un oiseau ne passe en fouettant de son aile
L'air épais, où circule un immense soleil.
Parfois quelque boa, chauffé dans son sommeil,
Fait onduler son dos dont l'écaille étincelle.

Tel l'espace enflammé brûle sous les cieux clairs.
Mais, tandis que tout dort aux mornes solitudes,
Les éléphants rugueux, voyageurs lents et rudes,
Vont au pays natal à travers les déserts.

D'un point de l'horizon, comme des masses brunes,
Ils viennent, soulevant la poussière, et l'on voit,
Pour ne pas dévier du chemin le plus droit,
Sous leur pied large et sûr crouler au loin les dunes.

Celui qui tient la tête est un vieux chef. Son corps
Est gercé comme un tronc que le temps ronge et mine;
Sa tête est comme un roc, et l'arc de son échine
Se voûte puissamment à ses moindres efforts.

The patriarch at a relentless pace
Guides to the certain goal his dusty band;
The massive pilgrims follow through the sand,
And in their wake a deep-ploughed furrow trace.

Their fan-shaped ears flap; trunks 'tween huge tusks swing,
And bellies throb and smoke; eyes closed they fare,
And clouds of sweat rise in the burning glare,
With storms of insects round them rioting.

What matters flies' voracity, and thirst,
And scorching sun that burns their wrinkled backs?
They dream of home forsaken, trampling tracks
To fig-tree forests where their race was nursed.

Once more they'll see the flood sprung from the steep,
Where swim the blaring hippopotami,
Where, silhouetted on a moonlit sky,
They crashed down, crushing reeds and drinking deep.

Bravely they lumber on, and full of cheer,
A black line on the sand's immensity:
The waste resumes its immobility:
The vast slopes on the skyline disappear.

Translated by ALAN CONDER

Charles Leconte de Lisle (1818-1894) by the perfection of his poetry became the accepted leader of the Parnasse. *He first turned to the beauties of the ancient Greek myths and then to the primitive civilizations outside the Greco-Roman sphere. Among the many subjects treated in his later poems is that of wild animals, which he pictures in their native habitats. Les Éléphants, reproduced here, is one of the most famous of these pieces.*

Sans ralentir jamais et sans hâter sa marche,
Il guide au but certain ses compagnons poudreux;
Et, creusant par derrière un sillon sablonneux,
Les pèlerins massifs suivent leur patriarche.

L'oreille en éventail, la trompe entre les dents,
Ils cheminent, l'oeil clos. Leur ventre bat et fume,
Et leur sueur dans l'air embrasé monte en brume;
Et bourdonnent autour mille insectes ardents.

Mais qu'importent la soif et la mouche vorace,
Et le soleil cuisant leur dos noir et plissé?
Ils rêvent en marchant du pays délaissé,
Des forêts de figuiers où s'abrita leur race.

Ils reverront le fleuve échappé des grands monts,
Où nagent en mugissant l'hippopotame énorme,
Où, blanchis par la lune et projetant leur forme,
Ils descendaient pour boire en écrasant les joncs.

Aussi, pleins de courage et de lenteur, ils passent
Comme une ligne noire, au sable illimité;
Et le désert reprend son immobilité
Quand les lourds voyageurs à l'horizon s'effacent.

The Albatross

For entertainment, sailors sometimes take
The albatross, that great sea-bird who sweeps
Across the sky, slow consort in the wake
Of vessels moving on the rolling deep.

Thrown on the deck, the king of azure sky,
Ashamed to know that he no longer soars,
Drags at his sides, disheveled and awry,
His great white wings, bent back like trailing oars.

How gauche, that winged voyager, and how weak!
Just now so fair, how ugly and absurd!
One tries to thrust a pipe into his beak;
Another limps, to mock the grounded bird!

The Poet, like that monarch of the clouds,
To arrow and to storm alike defiant,
Exiled on earth among the jeering crowds,
Walks awkwardly because his wings are giant.

Translated by FRANCIS DUKE

Charles Baudelaire (1821-1867) is, a century after his death, one of the most beloved poets of all time. His tortured life was a never ending emotional struggle between good and evil. The title of his collection of poems, Les Fleurs du Mal *(The Flowers of Evil) is an evidence of this unrelenting harassment. Pure physical sensation is the stuff of much of his poetry. Baudelaire accepts suffering as a means of attaining beauty and truth. His ideal of artistic workmanship is evident in his dedication of* Les Fleurs du Mal *to Théophile Gautier, the "impeccable poet." In his development of the relationships between the senses* (correspondances), *in his use of symbols, and in his disdain of rhetoric, Baudelaire makes an important step toward Symbolism. It should be recalled that Baudelaire found in Edgar Allan Poe a kindred spirit and that he translated some of Poe's works into French.*

L'Albatros

Souvent, pour s'amuser, les hommes d'équipage
Prennent des albatros, vastes oiseaux des mers,
Qui suivent, indolents compagnons de voyage,
Le navire glissant sur les gouffres amers.

À peine les ont-ils déposés sur les planches,
Que ces rois de l'azur, maladroits et honteux,
Laissent piteusement leurs grandes ailes blanches
Comme des avirons traîner à côté d'eux.

Ce voyageur ailé, comme il est gauche et veule!
Lui, naguère si beau, qu'il est comique et laid!
L'un agace son bec avec un brûle-gueule,
L'autre mime, en boitant, l'infirme qui volait!

Le Poète est semblable au prince des nuées
Qui hante la tempête et se rit de l'archer;
Exilé sur le sol au milieu des huées,
Ses ailes de géant l'empêchent de marcher.

Correspondences

From living piers of Nature's holy place,
Sometimes a muttering of vague words escapes.
Man walks through forests of symbolic shapes
Whose glances tell him of their kindred race.

As long, far echoes meet in common bond,
And in profound and shadowy unity
Enormous as the night or clarity,
So scent and sound and color correspond.

As cool as babies' flesh are some perfumes,
Sweet as an oboe, verdant as a lawn.
Others, corruption's rich, triumphant fumes,

In bold expansion to each other drawn,
Like musk and benzoin, amber and incense,
United to sing the joys of soul and sense.

Translated by FRANCIS DUKE

Correspondances

La Nature est un temple où de vivants piliers
Laissent parfois sortir de confuses paroles;
L'homme y passe à travers des forêts de symboles
Qui l'observent avec des regards familiers.

Comme de longs échos qui de loin se confondent
Dans une ténébreuse et profonde unité,
Vaste comme la nuit et comme la clarté,
Les parfums, les couleurs et les sons se répondent.

Il est des parfums frais comme des chairs d'enfants,
Doux comme les hautbois, verts comme les prairies,
— Et d'autres, corrompus, riches et triomphants,

Ayant l'expansion des choses infinies,
Comme l'ambre, le musc, le benjoin et l'encens,
Qui chantent les transports de l'esprit et des sens.

Evening Harmony

The time has come when, on its stem vibrating,
Each flower, like censers, spreads perfumes divine;
In twilit air, sounds and scents intertwine
Through swooning waltzes, sad and enervating!

Each flower, like censers, spreads perfumes divine;
Like swollen hearts the violin is pulsating
Through swooning waltzes, sad and enervating!
The sky is like a sad, fair wayside shrine.

Like swollen hearts the violin is pulsating,
Soft heart, that in black solitude must pine!
The sky is like a sad, fair wayside shrine;
The sun is drowned in blood coagulating.

Soft heart, that in black solitude must pine,
Bright memories of old accumulating,
The sun is drowned in blood coagulating . . .
In me, your memories like a monstrance shine!

Translated by FRANCIS DUKE

Harmonie du Soir

Voici venir les temps où vibrant sur sa tige
Chaque fleur s'évapore ainsi qu'un encensoir;
Les sons et les parfums tournent dans l'air du soir;
Valse mélancolique et langoureux vertige!

Chaque fleur s'évapore ainsi qu'un encensoir;
Le violon frémit comme un coeur qu'on afflige;
Valse mélancolique et langoureux vertige!
Le ciel est triste et beau comme un grand reposoir.

Le violon frémit comme un coeur qu'on afflige,
Un coeur tendre, qui hait le néant vaste et noir!
Le ciel est triste et beau comme un grand reposoir;
Le soleil s'est noyé dans son sang qui se fige …

Un coeur tendre, qui hait le néant vaste et noir,
Du passé lumineux recueille tout vestige!
Le soleil s'est noyé dans son sang qui se fige …
Ton souvenir en moi luit comme un ostensoir!

Spleen (II)

I've more than millenarian memories stored.

A bureau's drawers, with their encumbering hoard
Of balance-sheets, love-letters, verses, writs,
And dusty curls in old receipted chits,
Hold fewer secrets than my wretched head,
That pyramid, that cavern, where the dead
Closer than in a potter's field are strewn.

—I am a burial ground shunned by the moon,
Where, like remorse, long earthworms drag their way,
And always make my dearest dead their prey.
I am a dressing-room, long antiquated,
Its roses past their bloom, its clothes outdated,
With only pale Bouchers and shy pastels
Who still inhale the uncorked perfume's smells.

There is no tedium like the torpid flow
Of those days, smothered as by drifts of snow,
When boredom born of stupid apathy
Drags on as slow as all eternity.

—O living clay! henceforth you are no more
Than some granitic outcrop round which soar
Vague fears, who brood midst desert haze alone,
Old sphinx, to an indifferent world unknown,
Unmapped, and too morose your song to raise
Save only to the sunset's fading rays.

Translated by FRANCIS DUKE

Spleen II

J'ai plus de souvenirs que si j'avais mille ans.

Un gros meuble à tiroirs encombré de bilans,
De vers, de billets doux, de procès, de romances,
Avec de lourds cheveux roulés dans des quittances,
Cache moins de souvenirs que mon triste cerveau.
C'est une pyramide, un immense caveau,
Qui contient plus de morts que la fosse commune.

— Je suis un cimetière abhorré de la lune,
Où, comme des remords, se traînent de longs vers
Qui s'acharnent toujours sur mes morts les plus chers.
Je suis un vieux boudoir plein de roses fanées,
Où gît tout un fouillis de modes surannées,
Où les pastels plaintifs et les pâles Boucher,
Seuls, respirent l'odeur d'un flacon débouché.

Rien n'égale en longueur les boiteuses journées,
Quand sous les lourds flocons des neigeuses années
L'Ennui, fruit de la morne incuriosité,
Prend les proportions de l'immortalité.

— Désormais tu n'es plus, ô matière vivante!
Qu'un granit entouré d'une vague épouvante,
Assoupi dans le fond d'un Sahara brumeux!
Un vieux sphinx ignoré du monde insoucieux,
Oublié sur la carte, et dont l'humeur farouche
Ne chante qu'aux rayons du soleil qui se couche!

Self-Communion

Hush, Sorrow! Here comes Evening into sight,
As you wished, drifting down and drawing near,
His shadows wrapping all the city tight,
And bringing care to some, to others cheer.

While servile throngs of humans, taking flight
From Pleasure, iron-handed overseer,
Eat slaves' bread, tasting gall in every bite,
Take my hand, Sorrow, and come with me here

Away. In antiquated finery, see
The old Years lean from Heaven's balcony,
Regret surge smiling from the watery deeps,

The Sun's eye close in sleep beneath an arch;
And, as enshrouded from the East she creeps,
Listen, my dear, to Night's soft-footed march.

Translated by FRANCIS DUKE

Recueillement

Sois sage, ô ma Douleur, et tiens-toi plus tranquille.
Tu réclamais le Soir; il descend; le voici:
Une atmosphère obscure enveloppe la ville,
Aux uns portant la paix, aux autres le souci.

Pendant que des mortels la multitude vile,
Sous le fouet du Plaisir, ce bourreau sans merci,
Va cueillir des remords dans la fête servile,
Ma Douleur, donne-moi la main; viens par ici,

Loin d'eux. Vois se pencher les défuntes Années,
Sur les balcons du ciel, en robes surannées;
Surgir du fond des eaux le Regret souriant;

Le Soleil moribond s'endormir sous une arche,
Et, comme un long linceul traînant à l'Orient,
Entends, ma chère, entends la douce Nuit qui marche.

Invitation to Travel

My sister, my child,
How life would have smiled
At us two, together, down there,
In love at each breath,
In love until death,
In that land whose nature you share!
Whose suns, in their shrouds
Of scudding wet clouds
Arouse in my heart the same cheer,
The same charmed surprise,
As your fickle eyes
When sparkles dart forth through a tear!

There, beauty and harmony dwell
Where springs of voluptuousness well.

There, furniture, bright
With age-mellowed light,
Would shine in the depths of our chamber.
The rarest of blooms
Would blend their perfumes
With vague emanations of amber.
The ceilings' rich beams,
The mirrors' bright gleams,
The splendors that tell of the East,
Would all speak, apart,
To a harkening heart,
The sounds of a voice that had ceased.

There, beauty and harmony dwell
Where springs of voluptuousness well.

L'Invitation au Voyage

Mon enfant, ma soeur,
Songe à la douceur
D'aller là-bas vivre ensemble!
Aimer à loisir,
Aimer et mourir
Au pays qui te ressemble!
Les soleils mouillés
De ces ciels brouillés
Pour mon esprit ont les charmes
Si mystérieux
De tes traîtres yeux,
Brillant à travers leurs larmes.

Là, tout n'est qu'ordre et beauté,
Luxe, calme et volupté.

Des meubles luisants,
Polis par les ans,
Décoreraient notre chambre;
Les plus rares fleurs
Mêlant leurs odeurs
Aux vagues senteurs de l'ambre,
Les riches plafonds,
Les miroirs profonds,
La spendeur orientale,
Tout y parlerait
A l'âme en secret
Sa douce langue natale.

Là, tout n'est qu'ordre et beauté,
Luxe, calme et volupté.

In basins secured,
See all the ships moored
Who'd gladly be gone from their berth;
It's only to do
A favor to you,
They've come from the ends of the earth.
The setting suns shed
Their glory of red
On canals, fields, and town; and a flow
Of purple and gold
The world to enfold
In a warmly enveloping glow.

There, beauty and harmony dwell
Where springs of voluptuousness well.

Translated by FRANCIS DUKE

Vois sur ces canaux
Dormir ces vaisseaux
Dont l'humeur est vagabonde;
C'est pour assouvir
Ton moindre désir
Qu'ils viennent du bout du monde.
— Les soleils couchants
Revêtent les champs,
Les canaux, la ville entière,
D'hyacinthe et d'or;
Le monde s'endort
Dans une chaude lumière.

Là, tout n'est qu'ordre et beauté,
Luxe, calme et volupté.

The Little Flower Girl

The cold sun was giving a pink tint to the sleet,
And the November sky made one think of April.
We wanted to enjoy the fine frosty weather.
Myself very warmly dressed, you all bundled up
In a coat, wearing a small veil, and some warm gloves,
We were crossing, among the elegant couples,
Beneath the arch of the white, joyous avenue,
When suddenly up to us a girl lightly dressed
And blue with cold, some little flowers in her hand,
Came running, in great haste making herself a path
Among the well-dressed men and richly gowned ladies,
To offer us a small bouquet of violets.
She had divined that we were happy, without doubt,
And had said to herself, "They will be generous."
In a soft voice she asked us to buy her flowers,
While smiling with the smile of a child who is ill.
Alas, it was monstrous, this child of seven years
Who was dying of winter while offering spring.
Her poor little fingers were covered with chilblains.
I could smell the delicate perfume of your furs,
I could see your neck pink and white beneath your scarf,
And I could touch your hand that was warm in your muff.
We made our offering, my dear, and went on;
But gaiety had flown; our afflicted hearts
Were full 'til evening with that bitter memory.

My darling, we will do some good works this winter.

Translated by K. F. C.

François Coppée (1842-1908) is remembered today primarily for his sympathetic and picturesque portraits of Paris and its poor.

La Petite Marchande de Fleurs

Le soleil froid donnait un ton rose au grésil,
Et le ciel de novembre avait des airs d'avril.
Nous voulions profiter de la belle gelée.
Moi chaudement vêtu, toi bien emmitouflée
Sous le manteau, sous la voilette et sous les gants,
Nous franchissions, parmi les couples élégants,
La porte de la blanche et joyeuses avenue,
Quand soudain jusqu'à nous une enfant presque nue
Et livide, tenant des fleurettes en main,
Accourut, se frayant à la hâte un chemin
Entre les beaux habits et les riches toilettes,
Nous offrir un petit bouquet de violettes.
Elle avait deviné que nous étions heureux
Sans doute, et s'était dit: « Ils seront généreux.»
Elle nous proposa ses fleurs d'une voix douce,
En souriant avec ce sourire qui tousse.
Et c'était monstrueux, cette enfant de sept ans
Qui mourait de l'hiver en offrant le printemps.
Ses pauvres petits doigts étaient pleins d'engelures.
Moi, je sentais le fin parfum de tes fourrures,
Je voyais ton cou rose et blanc sous la fanchon,
Et je touchais ta main chaude dans ton manchon.
Nous fîmes notre offrande, amie, et nous passâmes;
Mais la gaîté s'était envolée, et nos âmes
Gardèrent jusqu'au soir un souvenir amer.

Mignonne, nous ferons l'aumône cet hiver.

Stained Glass

This shrine has seen fair dames and barons high,
Splendent in azure, gold, and glistering pearl,
Bow 'neath prelatic hands that sanctify
The armorial pride of marquis and of earl.

They rode to chase with horn or clarion strain,
With sword held high and falcon at the wrist,
Or fared toward distant lands, as to a tryst,
Where paynim cities front the Orient main.

Today these lords and their proud chatelaines,
With couchant greyhounds leashed in carven chains,
On lofty tombs of marble, black and white,

Lie moveless, voiceless, lapped in leaden dreams,
Turning their stony eyeballs, void of sight,
Toward the rose-window where the sunlight streams.

Translated by WILLIAM FREDERIC GIESE

José-Maria de Heredia (1842-1905) was born in Cuba, reputedly a descendant of Spanish conquistadores. After being educated in Paris, Heredia spent his whole life in literary pursuits. He was a most faithful disciple of Leconte de Lisle. His principal work is a series of 118 sonnets called Les Trophées *in which the very erudite writer seeks to perpetuate glorious memories of history, beginning with Ancient Greece.*

Le Vitrail

Cette verrière a vu dames et hauts barons
Étincelants d'azur, d'or, de flamme et de nacre,
Incliner sous la dextre auguste qui consacre,
L'orgueil de leurs cimiers et de leurs chaperons;

Lorsqu'ils allaient, au bruit du cor et des clairons,
Ayant le glaive au poing, le gerfaut ou le sacre,
Vers la plaine ou le bois, Byzance ou Saint-Jean d'Acre,
Partir pour la croisade ou le vol des hérons.

Aujourd'hui, les seigneurs auprès des châtelaines,
Avec le lévrier à leurs longues poulaines,
S'allongent aux carreaux de marbre blanc et noir;

Ils gisent là sans voix, sans geste et sans ouïe,
Et de leurs yeux de pierre ils regardent sans voir
La rose du vitrail toujours épanouie.

Autumn Song

The heavy thrall
Of the sobbing call
    Of the fall
Weighs, nor departs
Like my heart's
    Pall.

Overcome
And dumb,
    As the hours creep
I see the haze
Of olden days
    and weep.

And I go away
The wind's prey,
    In barren, brief
Whirl hither and yon
Like a wan
    Dead leaf.

Translated by JOSEPH T. SHIPLEY

Like Baudelaire, Paul Verlaine (1844-1896), led a life filled with torment, and, like his fellow poet, Verlaine produced some of the most hauntingly beautiful poetry in the French language. The music of poetry was his prime concern. He often uses verses of an odd number of syllables and combines them with verses of an even number. He changes the accentuation in the traditional alexandrine. He experiments with rhyme. In reading a poem of Verlaine, one feels that he is really reading a song. Verlaine's poems suggest more than they express, and his appeal is more to the emotions than to the mind.

Chanson d'Automne

Les sanglots longs
Des violons
  De l'automne
Blessent mon coeur
D'une langueur
  Monotone.

Tout suffocant
Et blême, quand
  Sonne l'heure,
Je me souviens
Des jours anciens
  Et je pleure.

Et je m'en vais
Au vent mauvais
  Qui m'emporte
Deçà, delà,
Pareil à la
  Feuille morte.

Il Pleut Doucement sur la Ville

Tears fall within mine heart,
As rain upon the town:
Whence does this languor start,
Possessing all mine heart?

O sweet fall of the rain
Upon the earth and roof,
Unto an heart in pain,
O music of the rain.

Tears that have no reason
Fall in my sorry heart:
What, there was no treason?
This grief hath no reason.

Nay, the more desolate,
Because, I know not why,
(Neither for love nor hate)
Mine heart is desolate.

Translated by ERNEST DOWSON

Il Pleure dans mon Coeur

Il pleure dans mon coeur
Comme il pleut sur la ville,
Quelle est cette langueur
Qui pénètre mon coeur?

O bruit doux de la pluie
Par terre et sur les toits!
Pour un coeur qui s'ennuie
O le chant de la pluie!

Il pleure sans raison
Dans ce coeur qui s'écoeure.
Quoi! nulle trahison?
Ce deuil est sans raison.

C'est bien la pire peine
De ne savoir pourquoi,
Sans amour et sans haine,
Mon coeur a tant de peine.

The Sky Is Up Above the Roof

The sky is up above the roof
      So blue, so soft.
A tree there, up above the roof,
      Swayeth aloft.

A bell within that sky we see,
      Chimes low and faint;
A bird upon that tree we see,
      Maketh complaint.

Dear God, is not the life up there
      Simple and sweet?
How peacefully are borne up there
      Sounds of the street.

What hast thou done, who comest here,
      To weep alway?
Where hast thou laid, who comest here,
      Thy youth away?

Translated by ERNEST DOWSON

Le Ciel est par-dessus le Toit

Le ciel est, par-dessus le toit,
        Si bleu, si calme!
Un arbre, par-dessus le toit,
        Berce sa palme.

La cloche, dans le ciel qu'on voit,
        Doucement tinte.
Un oiseau sur l'arbre qu'on voit
        Chante sa plainte.

Mon Dieu, mon Dieu, la vie est là,
        Simple et tranquille.
Cette paisible rumeur-là
        Vient de la ville.

— Qu'as-tu fait, ô toi que voilà
        Pleurant sans cesse,
Dis, qu'as-tu fait, toi que voilà,
        De ta jeunesse?

Art Poétique

Music first and foremost of all!
Choose your measure of odd not even,
Let it melt in the air of heaven,
Pose not, poise not, but rise and fall.

Choose your words, but think not whether
Each to other of old belong:
What so dear as the dim gray song
Where clear and vague are joined together?

'Tis veils of beauty for beautiful eyes,
'Tis the trembling light of the naked noon,
'Tis a medley of blue and gold, the moon
And stars in the cool of autumn skies.

Let every shape of its shade be born;
Color, away! come to me, shade!
Only of shade can the marriage be made
Of dream with dream and of flute with horn.

Shun the Point, lest death with it come,
Unholy laughter and cruel wit
(For the eyes of the angels weep at it)
And all the garbage of scullery-scum.

Take Eloquence, and wring the neck of him!
You had better, by force, from time to time,
Put a little sense in the head of Rhyme:
If you watch him not, you will be at the beck of him.

Art Poétique

De la musique avant toute chose,
Et pour cela préfère l'Impair
Plus vague et plus soluble dans l'air,
Sans rien en lui qui pèse ou qui pose.

Il faut aussi que tu n'ailles point
Choisir tes mots sans quelque méprise:
Rien de plus cher que la chanson grise
Où l'Indécis au Précis se joint.

C'est des beaux yeux derrière des voiles,
C'est le grand jour tremblant de midi,
C'est par un ciel d'automne attiédi,
Le bleu fouillis des claires étoiles!

Car nous voulons la Nuance encor,
Pas la Couleur, rien que la nuance!
Oh! la nuance seule fiance
Le rêve au rêve et la flûte au cor!

Fuis du plus loin la Pointe assassine,
L'Esprit cruel et le Rire impur,
Qui font pleurer les yeux de l'Azur,
Et tout cet ail de basse cuisine!

Prends l'éloquence et tords-lui son cou!
Tu feras bien, en train d'énergie,
De rendre un peu la Rime assagie,
Si l'on n'y veille, elle ira jusqu'où?

O, who shall tell us the wrongs of Rhyme?
What witless savage or what deaf boy
Has made for us this two-penny toy
Who bells ring hollow and out of time?

Music always and music still!
Let your verse be the wandering thing
That flutters in the light from a soul on the wing
Towards other skies at a new whim's will.

Let your verse be the luck of the lure
Afloat on the winds that at morning hint
Of the odors of thyme and the savor of mint . . .
And all the rest is literature.

Translated by ARTHUR SYMONS

Oh! qui dira les torts de la Rime?
Quel enfant sourd ou quel nègre fou
Nous a forgé ce bijou d'un sou
Qui sonne creux et faux sous la lime?

De la musique encore et toujours!
Que ton vers soit la chose envolée
Qu'on sent qui fuit d'une âme en allée
Vers d'autres cieux à d'autres amours.

Que ton vers soit la bonne aventure
Éparse au vent crispé du matin
Qui va fleurant la menthe et le thym . . .
Et tout le reste est littérature.

Green

I give these flowers and fruits, these leafy sprays,
And my heart also, throbbing for your sake,
Into your two white hands—oh, do not break
Such poor gifts, nor your eyes deny them praise.

I come all covered yet with dew the breeze
Of morning turns to ice upon my face.
Let my weariness, before your knees,
Dream these dear moments which will give it peace.

Let my head, still ringing with your last
Kisses, settle on your soft young breast;
And when the splendid hurricane has passed,
Perhaps I'll sleep a little while you rest.

Translated by C. F. MacIntyre

Green

Voici des fruits, des fleurs, des feuilles et des branches
Et puis voici mon coeur, qui ne bat que pour vous.
Ne le déchirez pas avec vos deux mains blanches
Et qu'à vos yeux si beaux l'humble présent soit doux.

J'arrive tout couvert encore de rosée
Que le vent du matin vient glacer à mon front.
Souffrez que ma fatigue, à vos pieds reposée,
Rêve des chers instants qui la délasseront.

Sur votre jeune sein laissez rouler ma tête
Toute sonore encor de vos derniers baisers;
Laissez-la s'apaiser de la bonne tempête,
Et que je dorme un peu puisque vous reposez.

Sensation

On sunny evenings I shall wander down a bridle-path,
The tall corn-blades will fondle me the while I tramp the turf;
And dreaming, I shall feel the chilly sweetness on my idle path,
And as a wave the wind shall lave my naked brow like surf.

I shall not speak a word, no thought shall fill the heart or head of me,
But love shall flow and fill my soul with its o'er-brimming tide;
And I shall wander far away, a gipsy in the tread of me,
As happy there with Nature fair as lover with his bride.

Translated by WILFRID THORLEY

Jean-Nicolas-Arthur Rimbaud (1854-1891) is a prime example of precocious genius in revolt. By age seventeen he had not only managed to be recognized at school as a brilliant scholar, he had also run away several times from his very strict family home, had written a good number of his most famous poems, including Bateau Ivre, *had formulated in great detail his poetics, and had aroused the enthusiasm of Verlaine to the point where the latter invited the young poet to join him in Paris. By the time he was twenty, Rimbaud had completed his poetic career. Yet, with Verlaine and Mallarmé, he stands in the forefront of the Symbolist movement. He believed that the poet had to develop a superhuman vision through ineffable torture, arrive at the unknown, and interpret it. His very emotional and imaginative impressions of the most traditional things can be seen in* Voyelles *in which he ascribes colors, sounds, odors, striking forms, and emotions to the vowels of the alphabet.*

Sensation

Par les soirs d'été bleus j'irai dans les sentiers,
Picoté par les blés, fouler l'herbe menue:
Rêveur, j'en sentirai la fraîcheur à mes pieds,
Je laisserai le vent baigner ma tête nue!

Je ne parlerai pas, je ne penserai rien.
Mais l'amour infini me montera dans l'âme;
Et j'irai loin, bien loin, comme un bohémien,
Par la Nature, — heureux comme avec une femme.

Head of a Faun

In the leafage, verdant casket stained with gold,
In the flowering, vague and changing greenery,
'Mid glowing blooms where sleeps the kiss, behold!
Thrust living through the lovely tracery

Is seen a stray faun's head; his brown eyes shine,
His white teeth bite red flowers; a moment after,
Tawny and bleeding as a ripe old wine,
Beneath the boughs his lips burst into laughter.

And when—like a silent squirrel—he has gone,
His laughter trembles still among the leaves,
—And, scared by a bullfinch piping, one perceives
Gold Kiss-o'-the-Wood, in self-communion.

Translated by ALAN CONDER

Tête de Faune

Dans la feuillée, écrin vert taché d'or,
Dans la feuillée incertaine et fleurie
De splendides fleurs où le baiser dort,
Vif et crevant l'exquise broderie,

Un faune effaré montre ses deux yeux
Et mord les fleurs rouges de ses dents blanches:
Brunie et sanglante ainsi qu'un vin vieux,
Sa lèvre éclate en rires sous les branches.

Et quand il a fui — tel qu'un écureuil, —
Son rire tremble encore à chaque feuille,
Et l'on voit épeuré par un bouvreuil
Le Baiser d'or du Bois, qui se recueille.

The Sleeper of the Valley

There's a green hollow where a river sings,
Silvering the torn grass in its glittering flight,
And where the sun from the proud mountain flings
Fire—and the little valley brims with light.

A soldier young, with open mouth, bare head,
Sleeps with his neck in dewy watercress,
Under the sky and on the grass his bed,
Pale in the deep green and the light's excess.

He sleeps amid the iris and his smile
Is like a sick child's slumbering for a while.
Nature, in thy warm lap his chilled limbs hide!

The perfume does not thrill him from his rest.
He sleeps in sunshine, hand upon his breast,
Tranquil—with two red holes in his right side.

Translated by LUDWIG LEWISOHN

Le Dormeur du Val

C'est un trou de verdure où chante une rivière
Accrochant follement aux herbes des haillons
D'argent, où le soleil, de la montagne fière,
Luit; c'est un petit val qui mousse de rayons.

Un soldat jeune, bouche ouverte, tête nue
Et la nuque baignant dans le frais cresson bleu,
Dort: il est étendu dans l'herbe, sous la nue,
Pâle dans son lit vert où la lumière pleut.

Les pieds dans les glaïeuls, il dort. Souriant comme
Sourirait un enfant malade, il fait un somme.
Nature, berce-le chaudement: il a froid!

Les parfums ne font pas frissonner sa narine;
Il dort dans le soleil, la main sur sa poitrine
Tranquille. Il a deux trous rouges au côté droit.

Vowels

Black *A*, white *E*, red *I*, green *U*, blue *O*,
Some day I'll tell your birth's dark mysteries.
First *A*, black hairy corselet of bright flies
Round deathly smells, dark gulfs of vertigo;

E, silver mists, proud glaciers, white kings, tents,
Belled snow flowers shuddering with frigid fire;
I, blood and crimsons, laugh of lips in ire
Or in the drunken trance of penitents;

U, orbits, heavenly throb of glaucous seas,
And peace of fields and kine, alchemic peace
Of graven lines on foreheads of the wise;

And *O*, last Trumpet, strange and strident, *O*,
The silence through which Worlds and Angels go:
—*O*, Omega, the azure of His Eyes!

Translated by ALAN CONDER

Voyelles

A noir, *E* blanc, *I* rouge, *U* vert, *O* bleu, voyelles,
Je dirai quelque jour vos naissances latentes.
A, noir corset velu des mouches éclatantes
Qui bombillent autour des puanteurs cruelles,

Golfe d'ombre; *E,* candeur des vapeurs et des tentes,
Lance des glaciers fiers, rois blancs, frissons d'ombelles;
I, pourpre, sang craché, rire des lèvres belles
Dans la colère ou les ivresses pénitentes;

U, cycles, vibrements divins des mers virides,
Paix des pâtis semés d'animaux, paix des rides
Que l'alchimie imprime aux grands fronts studieux;

O, suprême clairon plein de strideurs étranges,
Silences traversés des Mondes et des Anges:
— *O* l'Oméga, rayon violet de Ses Yeux!

Wind From the Sea

Weary is the flesh, alas! with many books the eyes are dim.
Flight! I feel that birds are wild to sweep the far-off skies, and skim
The unknown foam! For nought on land shall now the gypsy heart
    be stayed,
Not ancient gardens mirrored back by limpid eyes, since it doth wade
Into the sea-borne flood. O nights! not the clear lamplight's lonely tryst,
Nor white allure of sheets unscrawled, nor yet the suckling infant kist
By the young wife. I must away! The steamer rocks her ropes and spars!
O haul the heavy anchor up and set all sail for tropic stars!
Now weariness at last outworn by ruthless hope's unsparing whip
Still strains toward white handkerchiefs that wave their farewells
    from the ship.
Nay, but these masts that brave the storm, may they not bend above
    the foam
Like wind-broke spars on derelicts that mastless drift far, far from home
Or happy haven-isles that flow with wine and oil that never fails? . . .
But hearken, O my heart, the singing mariners that hoist the sails!

Translated by WILFRID THORLEY

Stéphane Mallarmé (1842-1898) is called the master of the Symbolist school. To earn a living Mallarmé taught English in various lycées, *but his life was devoted to poetry. His Tuesday evening receptions at home in the* rue de Rome *in Paris were attended by many writers who have become famous in French literature. Mallarmé was first inspired by Baudelaire in* Les Fleurs du Mal *and by Edgar Allan Poe whose* The Raven *he translated into French. As Mallarmé's poetry evolved, it became more and more subtle and complex. He thought of poetry as sacred and enveloped it in mystery so that only the devoted disciple would struggle to pierce its meaning. Claude Debussy's famous prelude was inspired by Mallarmé's* L'Après-midi d'un Faune.

Brise Marine

La chair est triste, hélas! et j'ai lu tous les livres.
Fuir! là-bas fuir! Je sens que des oiseaux sont ivres
D'être parmi l'écume inconnue et les cieux!
Rien, ni les vieux jardins reflétés par les yeux
Ne retiendra ce cœur qui dans la mer se trempe
Ô nuits! ni la clarté déserte de ma lampe
Sur le vide papier que la blancheur défend
Et ni la jeune femme allaitant son enfant.
Je partirai! Steamer balancant ta mâture,
Lève l'ancre pour une exotique nature!
Un Ennui, désolé par les cruels espoirs,
Croit encore à l'adieu suprême des mouchoirs!
Et, peut-être, les mâts, invitant les orages,
Sont-ils de ceux qu'un vent penche sur les naufrages
Perdus, sans mâts, sans mâts, ni fertiles îlots . . .
Mais, ô mon coeur, entends le chant des matelots!

Sigh

My soul, calm sister, towards thy brow, whereon scarce grieves
An autumn strewn already with its russet leaves,
And towards the wandering sky of thine angelic eyes,
Mounts, as in melancholy gardens may arise
Some faithful fountain sighing whitely towards the blue!
Towards the blue, pale and pure, that sad October knew,
When, in those depths, it mirrored languors infinite,
And agonizing leaves upon the waters white,
Windily drifting, traced a furrow cold and dun,
Where, in one long last ray, lingered the yellow sun.

Translated by ARTHUR SYMONS

Soupir

Mon âme, vers ton front où rêve, ô calme sœur,
Un automne jonché de taches de rousseur
Et vers le ciel errant de ton œil angélique
Monte, comme dans un jardin mélancolique,
Fidèle, un blanc jet d'eau soupire vers l'Azur!
— Vers l'Azur attendri d'octobre pâle et pur
Qui mire aux grands bassins sa langueur infinie
Et laisse sur l'eau morte où la fauve agonie
Des feuilles erre au vent et creuse un froid sillon,
Se traîner le soleil jaune d'un long rayon.

It Is the Good Hour

It is the good hour when the lamps appear,
The evening holds consoling calm for all,
And in the silence one could almost hear
A feather fall.

It is the good hour when, so sweetly,
Comes my well beloved to me,
Like a cloud, or zephyr free,
All sweetly, and all softly.

At first she's quiet—and I listen,
And her soul I recognize,
I see it sparkle out and glisten,
And I kiss her eyes.

It is the good hour when the lamps appear,
And the confessions
Of having loved each other all the day
From the heart's depths profound yet clear
Find their way.

And we talk of simple things,
The fruit we plucked in the garden;
The flower whose bloom was seen
Between the mosses green;
And the thought born, in sudden agitation,
At the memory of a faded word—my dear!—
Found at the bottom of an old desk drawer,
In a letter of another year.

Translated by MR. AND MRS. CLARK STILLMAN

C'est la Bonne Heure

C'est la bonne heure, où la lampe s'allume :
Tout est si calme et consolant, ce soir,
Et le silence est tel, que l'on entendrait choir
Des plumes.

C'est la bonne heure où, doucement,
S'en vient la bien aimée,
Comme la brise ou la fumée,
Tout doucement, tout lentement.

Elle ne dit rien d'abord — et je l'écoute ;
Et son âme, que j'entends toute,
Je la surprends luire et jaillir
Et je la baise sur ses yeux.

C'est la bonne heure, où la lampe s'allume,
Où les aveux
De s'être aimés le jour durant,
Du fond du cœur profond mais transparent,
S'exhument.

Et l'on se dit les simples choses :
Le fruit qu'on a cueilli dans le jardin ;
La fleur qui s'est ouverte,
D'entre les mousses vertes ;
Et la pensée éclose, en des émois soudains,
Au souvenir d'un mot de tendresse fanée
Surpris au fond d'un vieux tiroir,
Sur un billet de l'autre année.

Jeanne

Shepherdess born in Lorraine
Who, cotton-clad, guarded the sheep along the plain,
And who wept at the woes of the people of France
And led the King to Rheims with fluttering lance,
Jeanne, who are an arc, a cross, a sword, a heart, a spear,
Whom as father and mother the folk revere,
Jeanne, wounded and seized, to the English betrayed,
By the English at Rouen burned and displayed,
Jeanne, like unto an angel in wrath,
Jeanne d'Arc, set wrath in our hearts.

Translated by JOSEPH T. SHIPLEY

Rémy de Gourmont (1858-1915) is a man of many talents: poet, critic, dramatist, biologist, philosopher, novelist, philologist, and grammarian. His poetry is marked by great freedom in rhythm and rich imagery.

Jeanne

Bergère née en Lorraine,
Jeanne qui avez gardé les moutons en robe de futaine,
Et qui avez pleuré aux misères du peuple de France,
Et qui avez conduit le Roi à Reims parmi les lances,
Jeanne qui étiez un arc, une croix, un glaive, un cœur, une lance,
Jeanne que les gens aimaient comme leur père et leur mère,
Jeanne blessée et prise, mise au cachot par les Anglais,
Jeanne brûlée à Rouen par les Anglais,
Jeanne qui ressemblez à un ange en colère,
Jeanne d'Arc, mettez beaucoup de colère dans nos cœurs.

Autumn

Cowardly like the cold and rain,
Harsh and merciless like the wind,
Suspect and false like low hung sky,
Autumn is prowling in our midst,
His stick strikes against the shutters;
Open the door, for he is there.

Open the door and reproach him,
His mantle is frayed and dragging,
His feet are all heavy with mud;
Throw stones at him; whate'er he says
Have no fear for his words of hate:
It's only a rôle he's playing.

For I know him well, it is he
Who came last year with some stories,
With smiles and some bunches of grapes,
Talking of the good sun that shines,
Of the summer wind that whispers,
Of the sweet rest after travail.

He has supped at our festive board
—I know him full well, I tell you—
He has tasted the new pressed wine,
Then he has slept in the stable
Between the mare and the bull calf:
Next day the water was frozen,
The leaves had rained down from the frost.
—Now close the door and the shutters.

L'Automne

Lâche comme le froid et la pluie,
Brutal et sourd comme le vent,
Louche et faux comme le ciel bas,
L'Automne rôde par ici,
Son bâton heurte aux contrevents;
Ouvre la porte, car il est là.

Ouvre la porte et fais-lui honte,
Son manteau s'effiloche et traîne,
Ses pieds sont alourdis de boue;
Jette-lui des pierres, quoi qu'il te conte
Ne crains pas ses paroles de haine:
C'est toujours un rôle qu'il joue.

Car je le connais bien, c'est lui
Qui vint l'antan avec des phrases,
Avec des sourires et des grappes,
Parlant du bon soleil qui luit,
Du vent d'été qui bruit et jase,
Du bon repos après l'étape;

Il a soupé à notre table.
— Je le reconnais bien, te dis-je —
Il a goûté au vin nouveau,
Puis on l'a couché dans l'étable
Entre la jument et le veau:
Le lendemain l'eau était prise,
Les feuilles avaient plu sous la gelée.
— Ferme la porte et les volets.

Let him go on his way, at least,
And sleep elsewhere than in my hay.
Let him go begging farther on,
With his beard full of dead leaves
And his deep-set eyes that pierce you
And his hoarse and affected voice;
Away with him, I know him well,
Be he prettied up or in rags,
—Take in the bell, or he might ring!
Now make a bright fire, I await
Old winter with the honest face.

Translated by K. F. C.

Francis Vielé-Griffin (1864-1937) was born in Norfolk, Virginia. However, he went to France as a child and is always thought of as a French Symbolist poet. Vielé-Griffin lived especially in the Loire Valley and in the Dordogne. His poetry in large part concerns itself with nature and reflects the poet's experiments in free verse.

Qu'il passe son chemin, au moins,
Qu'il couche ailleurs que dans mon foin,
Qu'il aille mendier plus loin,
Avec des feuilles dans sa barbe
Et ses yeux creux qui vous regardent
Et sa voix rauque et doucereuse;
À d'autres! moi, je le reconnais,
Qu'il s'attife d'or ou qu'il gueuse.
— Rentre la cloche: s'il sonnait!
Prépare une flambée, j'attends
Le vieil hiver au regard franc.

The Dining Room

There is a rather dull cupboard here
that knew the voice of my great aunts,
that knew the voice of my grandfather dear,
that knew the voice of my father, too;
and to these memories it is true.
You're wrong to think it can only sit,
because I talk with it.

There's also a cuckoo made of wood.
I don't know why its voice is no longer good.
I don't like to ask . . . You see,
the voice might really be
broken, up there in its head,
just like the voice of the dead.

There's also an old buffet
that smells of wax and of conserve,
meat, and bread, and ripened pears.
It's a faithful servant and it swears
'twill all our goods preserve.

Lots of men and women have been here, near it,
who do not believe in such a spirit.
And I smile, when a visitor comes my way,
that he thinks me alone, and starts to say:
"Good morning, Mr. James, how are you today?"

Translated by JOSEPH T. SHIPLEY

Francis Jammes (1868-1938) is an independent poet of the Pyrenees region. His distinctive work is the result of careful observation, especially of nature, which he sets down with artistic simplicity. While Jammes early experimented with Symbolism and free verse, he returned to the classic verse form at about the time of his conversion to Catholicism in 1905 under the influence of Paul Claudel.

La Salle à Manger

Il y a une armoire à peine luisante
qui a entendu la voix de mes grand-tantes,
qui a entendu la voix de mon grand-père,
qui a entendu la voix de mon père.
À ces souvenirs l'armoire est fidèle.
On a tort de croire qu'elle ne sait que se taire,
car je cause avec elle.

Il y a aussi un coucou en bois.
Je ne sais pourqoi il n'a plus de voix.
Je ne veux pas le lui demander.
Peut-être bien qu'elle est cassée,
la voix qui était dans son ressort,
tout bonnement comme celle des morts.

Il y a aussi un vieux buffet
qui sent la cire, la confiture,
la viande, le pain et les poires mûres.
C'est un serviteur fidèle qui sait
qu'il ne doit rien nous voler.

Il est venu chez moi bien des hommes et des femmes
qui n'ont pas cru à ces petites âmes.
Et je souris que l'on me pense seul vivant
quand un visiteur me dit en entrant:
— Comment allez-vous, monsieur Jammes?

Helen, The Sad Queen

Azure, I come! from the caves of death withdrawn
To hear the waves break rhythmic on the shores,
To see swift galleys clear, across the dawn,
Lifting from darkness on the blades of golden oars.

My lonely hands now summon forth the kings
Whose salt-gray beards amuse my chaste fingers . . .
I wept . . . And each his gloomy triumph sings
And behind the stern of his bark the furrow lingers.

I hear sonorous conchs and clarion calls
Marking the lift of the oars and their even falls.
The clear chant of the undulant oarsmen charms

The tumult; and the gods! heroic at the prow,
With their olden smile and the spray hurled at their brow,
Stretch towards me their indulgent, graven arms.

Translated by JOSEPH T. SHIPLEY

Paul Valéry (1871-1945) was born of a Corsican father and Genoese mother. Poetry was one of his early interests, and the poems reprinted here are of this early period, but it is important to know that Valéry spent most of his life analyzing mental processes. In fact he filled more than two hundred fifty notebooks with observations on the phenomena of thinking. As private secretary to the director of the Agence Havas, *a great French news agency, for twenty-two years, Valéry was kept constantly in touch with world-wide happenings and at the same time had considerable leisure to pursue his own interests. He remained a close friend of Mallarmé and the group of writers that surrounded the master. Married to the niece of Berthe Morisot, Valéry was greatly interested in art. He was also an opera lover. In 1912 André Gide and Gaston Gallimard encouraged Valéry to publish his early poems. Revising these writings of his youth, Valéry was again carried away by his passion for the Muse, and during the following ten years he was to write his greatest poetic masterpieces.*

Hélène

Azur! c'est moi . . . Je viens des grottes de la mort
Entendre l'onde se rompre aux degrés sonores,
Et je revois les galères dans les aurores
Ressusciter de l'ombre au fil des rames d'or.

Mes solitaires mains appellent les monarques
Dont la barbe de sel amusait mes doigts purs;
Je pleurais. Ils chantaient leurs triomphes obscurs
Et les golfes enfuis des poupes de leurs barques,

J'entends les conques profondes et les clairons
Militaires rythmer le vol des avirons;
Le chant clair des rameurs enchaîne le tumulte,

Et les Dieux, à la proue héroïque exaltés
Dans leur sourire antique et que l'écume insulte
Tendent vers moi leurs bras indulgents et sculptés.

The Friendly Wood

We were thinking of things pure,
Side by side, along the paths,
We were holding hands
Without speaking . . . among the dark flowers.

We strolled like a couple betrothed,
Alone, in the green night of the fields,
Sharing the fruit of fairyland,
The moon friendly to madness.

And then we lay dead on the moss,
Far away, all alone, in the soft shadows
Of the intimate murmuring wood;

And above us, in the immense light,
We found ourselves weeping
Oh my dear companion of silence!

Translated by C. F. MacIntyre and James Laughlin

Le Bois Amical

Nous avons pensé des choses pures
Côte à côte, le long des chemins,
Nous nous sommes tenus par les mains
Sans dire . . . parmi les fleurs obscures;

Nous marchions comme des fiancés
Seuls, dans la nuit verte des prairies;
Nous partagions ce fruit de féeries
La lune amicale aux insensés

Et puis, nous sommes morts sur la mousse,
Très loin, tout seuls parmi l'ombre douce
De ce bois intime et murmurant;

Et là-haut, dans la lumière immense,
Nous nous sommes trouvés en pleurant
Ô mon cher compagnon de silence!

A Round

If all the girls in the world wanted to join hands,
all around the sea they could dance a round.
If all the boys in the world wanted to be sailors,
they would make with their ships a lovely bridge across the sea.
Then we could dance a round around the world,
if all the people in the world wanted to join hands.

Translated by K. F. C.

Paul Fort (1872-1906) is known for his free flowing, rhythmic ballads which look like prose and read like poetry. La Ronde, which is reproduced here, is universally used as a simple plea for world friendship.

La Ronde

Si toutes les filles du monde voulaient s'donner la main,
tout autour de la mer elles pourraient faire une ronde.

Si tous les gens du monde voulaient bien êtr' marins,
ils f'raient avec leurs barques un joli pont sur l'onde.

Alors on pourrait faire une ronde autour du monde,
Si tous les gens du monde voulaient s'donner la main.

The Cat

I want in my own home:
A wife of sound reason
A cat among the books
Friends in every season
Without which I cannot live.

Translated by ROGER SHATTUCK

Guillaume Apollinaire (Guglielmo-Apollinaris de Kostrowitzki)—(1880-1918) is one of the most interesting and controversial poets of our time. Born in Rome of a Polish mother and perhaps an Italian father, Apollinaire had his early education in Monaco where his mother was employed as entraîneuse *at the Casino. In 1901-02 he was employed as a tutor in Germany. Here he met Annie Playden, an English governess, the* Annie *of his early poems. In Paris he was a friend of Picasso, Derain, and Vlaminck and became interested in Cubism. His multiple love affairs are the subject of much of his poetry. Of the women in his life, the painter Marie Laurencin is the best known. Apollinaire's name is most often linked with the invention of the word* Surréalisme.

Le Chat

Je souhaite dans ma maison:
Une femme ayant sa raison,
Un chat passant parmi les livres,
Des amis en toute saison
Sans lesquels je ne peux pas vivre.

Annie

Between Mobile and Galveston
On the seacoast of Texas
There's a big garden full of rosebushes
And a house like a big rose.

Often there is a woman
Walking alone in the garden
And when I pass along the lime-bordered highway
We look at one another.

She is a Mennonite this woman
And her rosebushes and clothes are buttonless
I see that two buttons are missing from my jacket
The lady and I observe almost the same rite.

Translated by WILLIAM MEREDITH

Annie

Sur la côte du Texas
Entre Mobile et Galveston il y a
Un grand jardin tout plein de roses
Il contient aussi une villa
Qui est une grande rose

Une femme se promène souvent
Dans le jardin toute seule
Et quand je passe sur la route bordée de tilleuls
Nous nous regardons

Comme cette femme est mennonite
Ses rosiers et ses vêtements n'ont pas de boutons
Il en manque deux à mon veston
La dame et moi suivons presque le même rite

Smoke in the Canteen

(Poems to Lou)

Smoke in the canteen is like night descending
High pitched voices or low, wine running red as blood
I draw on my pipe, free and proud among my comrades
They will leave with me for the fields of battle
They will sleep at night in the rain or under the stars
They will gallop with me, bearing victories on horses' rumps
They will obey with me the same orders
They will listen with me to the sublime army bands
They will die near me and I perhaps near them
They will suffer from the cold and the sun with me
They obey with me the laws of man
They look at the women who go along the road
They want them, but I have more exalted loves
That reign over my heart, my senses, and my brain
And which are my country, my family, and my hope
For me, a soldier in love, a soldier of *la douce France*

Translated by K. F. C.

La Fumée de la Cantine

(Poèmes à Lou)

La fumée de la cantine est comme la nuit qui vient
Voix hautes ou graves le vin saigne partout
Je tire ma pipe libre et fier parmi mes camarades
Ils partiront avec moi pour les champs de bataille
Ils dormiront la nuit sous la plue ou les étoiles
Ils galoperont avec moi portant en croupe des victoires
Ils obéiront avec moi aux mêmes commandements
Ils écouteront attentifs les sublimes fanfares
Ils mourront près de moi et moi peut-être près d'eux
Ils souffriront du froid et du soleil avec moi
Ils sont des hommes ceux-ci qui boivent avec moi
Ils obéissent avec moi aux lois de l'homme
Ils regardent sur la route les femmes qui passent
Ils les désirent mais moi j'ai des plus hautes amours
Qui règnent sur mon cœur mes sens et mon cerveau
Et qui sont ma patrie ma famille et mon espérance
À moi soldat amoureux soldat de la douce France

Liberty

On my schoolboy's notebooks
On my desk and on the trees
On sand on snow
I write your name

On all pages read
On all blank pages
Stone blood paper or ash
I write your name

On gilded images
On the weapons of warriors
On the crowns of kings
I write your name

On jungle and desert
On nests on gorse
On the echo of my childhood
I write your name

On the wonders of nights
On the white bread of days
On betrothed seasons
I write your name

On all my rags of azure
On the pool musty sun
On the lake living moon
I write your name

Liberté

Sur mes cahiers d'écolier
Sur mon pupitre et les arbres
Sur le sable sur la neige
J'écris ton nom

Sur toutes les pages lues
Sur toutes les pages blanches
Pierre sang papier ou cendre
J'écris ton nom

Sur les images dorées
Sur les armes des guerriers
Sur la couronne des rois
J'écris ton nom

Sur la jungle et le désert
Sur les nids sur les genêts
Sur l'écho de mon enfance
J'écris ton nom

Sur les merveilles des nuits
Sur le pain blanc des journées
Sur les saisons fiancées
J'écris ton nom

Sur tous mes chiffons d'azur
Sur l'étang soleil moisi
Sur le lac lune vivante
J'écris ton nom

On fields on the horizon
On the wings of birds
And on the mill of shadows
I write your name

On each puff of dawn
On the sea on ships
On the demented mountain
I write your name

On the foam of clouds
On the sweat of storm
On thick insipid rain
I write your name

On shimmering shapes
On bells of color
On physical truth
I write your name

On awakened pathways
On roads spread out
On overflowing squares
I write your name

On the lamp that is lit
On the lamp that burns out
On my reunited houses
I write your name

On the fruit cut in two
Of the mirror and my chamber
On my bed empty shell
I write your name

Sur les champs sur l'horizon
Sur les ailes des oiseaux
Et sur le moulin des ombres
J'écris ton nom

Sur chaque bouffée d'aurore
Sur la mer sur les bateaux
Sur la montagne démente
J'écris ton nom

Sur la mousse des nuages
Sur les sueurs de l'orage
Sur la pluie épaisse et fade
J'écris ton nom

Sur les formes scintillantes
Sur les cloches des couleurs
Sur la vérité physique
J'écris ton nom

Sur les sentiers éveillés
Sur les routes déployées
Sur les places qui débordent
J'écris ton nom

Sur la lampe qui s'allume
Sur la lampe qui s'éteint
Sur mes maisons réunies
J'écris ton nom

Sur le fruit coupé en deux
Du miroir et de ma chambre
Sur mon lit coquille vide
J'écris ton nom

On my dog greedy and tender
On his trained ears
On his awkward paw
I write your name

On the springboard of my door
On familiar objects
On the flood of blessed fire
I write your name

On all tuned flesh
On the foreheads of my friends
On each hand outstretched
I write your name

On the window of surprises
On the attentive lips
Well above silence
I write your name

On my destroyed refuges
On my crumbled beacons
On the walls of my weariness
I write your name

On absence without desire
On naked solitude
On the steps of death
I write your name

On health returned
On the risk disappeared
On hope without memory
I write your name

Sur mon chien gourmand et tendre
Sur ses oreilles dressées
Sur sa patte maladroite
J'écris ton nom

Sur le tremplin de ma porte
Sur les objets familiers
Sur le flot du feu béni
J'écris ton nom

Sur toute chair accordée
Sur le front de mes amis
Sur chaque main qui se tend
J'écris ton nom

Sur la vitre des surprises
Sur les lèvres attentives
Bien au-dessus du silence
J'écris ton nom

Sur mes refuges détruits
Sur mes phares écroulés
Sur les murs de mon ennui
J'écris ton nom

Sur l'absence sans désir
Sur la solitude nue
Sur les marches de la mort
J'écris ton nom

Sur la santé revenue
Sur le risque disparu
Sur l'espoir sans souvenir
J'écris ton nom

And by the power of a word
I start my life again
I was born to know you
To name you

Liberty

Translated by LLOYD ALEXANDER

Paul Éluard (1895-1952) was first attracted by the techniques of Sur-
realism. By 1936 he had begun modifying his surrealism, however, to fit his
intense concern with the great social problems of his time. The Spanish Civil
War served only to deepen this engagement. During the Second World War
Éluard was very active in the Résistance and it was during this time that he
wrote Liberté, *which was circulated clandestinely and which became probably*
the most famous poem of the great resistance movement.

Et par le pouvoir d'un mot
Je recommence ma vie
Je suis né pour te connaître
Pour te nommer

Liberté

Homecoming

A Breton returns to his birthplace
After having pulled off several fast deals
He walks in front of the factories at Douarnenez
He recognizes nobody
Nobody recognizes him
He is very sad
He goes into a *crêpe* shop to eat some *crêpes*
But he can't eat any
There's something that keeps him from swallowing
He pays
He goes out
He lights a cigarette
But he can't smoke it
There's something
Something in his head
Something bad
He gets sadder and sadder
And suddenly he begins to remember:
Somebody told him when he was little
"You'll end up on the scaffold"
And for years
He never dared do anything
Not even cross the street
Not even go to sea
Nothing absolutely nothing.
He remembers.
The one who'd predicted everything was Uncle Grésillard
Uncle Grésillard who brought everybody bad luck
The swine!

Le Retour au Pays

(Paroles)

C'est un Breton qui revient au pays natal
Après avoir fait plusieurs mauvais coups
Il se promène devant les fabriques à Douarnenez
Il ne reconnaît personne
Personne ne le reconnaît
Il est très triste.
Il entre dans une crêperie pour manger des crêpes
Mais il ne peut pas en manger
Il a quelque chose qui les empêche de passer
Il paye
Il sort
Il allume une cigarette
Mais il ne peut pas la fumer.
Il y a quelque chose
Quelque chose dans sa tête
Quelque chose de mauvais
Il est de plus en plus triste
Et soudain il se met à se souvenir :
Quelqu'un lui a dit quand il était petit
« Tu finiras sur l'échafaud »
Et pendant des années
Il n'a jamais osé rien faire
Pas même traverser la rue
Pas même partir sur la mer
Rien absolument rien.
Il se souvient.
Celui qui avait tout prédit c'est l'oncle Grésillard
L'oncle Grésillard qui portait malheur à tout le monde
La vache

And the Breton thinks of his sister
Who works at Vaugirard,
Of his brother killed in the War
Thinks of all the things he's seen
All the things he's done.
Sadness grips him
He tries again
To light a cigarette
But he doesn't feel like smoking
So then he decides to go see Uncle Grésillard.
He goes.
He opens the door
Uncle doesn't recognize him
But he recognizes him
And he says to him
"Good morning Uncle Grésillard"
And then he wrings his neck
And he ends up on the scaffold at Quimper
After having eaten two dozen *crêpes*
And smoked a cigarette.

Translated by LAWRENCE FERLINGHETTI

Jacques Prévert (1900-   ) until recently was perhaps best known in the United States for his scenario of Les Enfants du Paradis, *the film, made in France during the Second World War, which featured Jean-Louis Barrault as pantomimist. Prévert might well be called a popular poet with surrealist overtones. In one vein he is a caricaturist-critic of the stupidities of our time. In another he is the sympathetic and sentimental painter of everyday life, writing in the picturesque language of the common man.*

Et le Breton pense à sa sœur
Qui travaille à Vaugirard
À son frère mort à la guerre
Pense à toutes les choses qu'il a vues
Toutes les choses qu'il a faites.
La tristesse se serre contre lui
Il essaie une nouvelle fois
D'allumer une cigarette
Mais il n'a pas envie de fumer
Alors il décide d'aller voir l'oncle Grésillard.
Il y va
Il ouvre la porte
L'oncle ne le reconnaît pas
Mais lui le reconnaît
Et il lui dit:
« Bonjour oncle Grésillard »
Et puis il lui tord le cou.
Et il finit sur l'échafaud à Quimper
Après avoir mangé deux douzaines de crêpes
Et fumé une cigarette.

Song of the Seine

(Spectacle)

The Seine has all the luck
She doesn't have a care
She just keeps gliding softly
Twenty-four hours a day
And she flows forth from her source
So sweetly without a sound
And without making a fuss
Without leaving her bed
She goes on toward the sea
While passing through Paree

The Seine has all the luck
She doesn't have a care
And when she goes for a stroll
All the length of her quays
With her handsome robe of green
And her soft golden lights
Notre-Dame so jealous
Motionless and severe
From the top of all her stones
Looks at her with cold disdain
But the Seine takes it all lightly
She doesn't have a care
She just keeps gliding softly
Twenty-four hours a day
And goes off toward Le Havre
And goes off toward the sea
While passing like a dream
In the midst of the mysteries
Of the miseries of Paree.

Translated by K. F. C.

JACQUES PRÉVERT

Chanson de la Seine

(Spectacle)

La Seine a de la chance
Elle n'a pas de soucis
Elle se la coule douce
Le jour comme la nuit
Et elle sort de sa source
Tout doucement sans bruit
Et sans se faire de mousse
Sans sortir de son lit
Elle s'en va vers la mer
En passant par Paris

La Seine a de la chance
Elle n'a pas de soucis
Et quand elle se promène
Tout le long de ses quais
Avec sa belle robe verte
Et ses lumières dorées
Notre-Dame jalouse
Immobile et sévère
Du haut de toutes ses pierres
La regarde de travers
Mais la Seine s'en balance
Elle n'a pas de soucis
Elle se la coule douce
Le jour comme la nuit
Et s'en va vers le Havre
Et s'en va vers la mer
En passant comme un rêve
Au mil des mystères
Des misères de Paris.

So Many Forests

(Rain and Fine Weather)

So many forests torn out of the earth
and massacred
done in
rolled flat

So many forests sacrificed for paper pulp
billions of newspapers drawing annually
    the attention of readers to the denudation
    of the woods and forests.

Translated by K. F. C.

Tant de Forêts

(La Pluie et le Beau Temps)

Tant de forêts arrachées à la terre
et massacrées
achevées
rotativées

Tant de forêts sacrifiées pour la pâte à papier
des milliards de journaux attirant annuellement l'attention des lecteurs sur le danger du déboisement des
bois et des forêts.